Risking NATO

Testing the Limits of the Alliance in Afghanistan

Andrew R. Hoehn, Sarah Harting

Prepared for the United States Air Force

Approved for public release; distribution unlimited

PROJECT AIR FORCE

The research described in this report was sponsored by the United States Air Force under Contract FA7014-06-C-0001. Further information may be obtained from the Strategic Planning Division, Directorate of Plans, Hq USAF.

Library of Congress Cataloging-in-Publication Data

Hoehn, Andrew R.
  Risking NATO : testing the limits of the alliance in Afghanistan / Andrew R. Hoehn, Sarah Harting.
    p. cm.
  Includes bibliographical references.
  ISBN 978-0-8330-5011-3 (pbk. : alk. paper)
      1. North Atlantic Treaty Organization—Afghanistan—Operations other than war. 2. North Atlantic Treaty Organization—Armed Forces—Afghanistan. 3. North Atlantic Treaty Organization—Afghanistan. 4. Afghan War, 2001- I. Harting, Sarah. II. Title.

  UA646.3.H59 2010
  958.104'73091821—dc22

2010044237

The RAND Corporation is a nonprofit institution that helps improve policy and decisionmaking through research and analysis. RAND's publications do not necessarily reflect the opinions of its research clients and sponsors.

RAND® is a registered trademark.

Published 2010 by the RAND Corporation
1776 Main Street, P.O. Box 2138, Santa Monica, CA 90407-2138
1200 South Hayes Street, Arlington, VA 22202-5050
4570 Fifth Avenue, Suite 600, Pittsburgh, PA 15213-2665
RAND URL: http://www.rand.org/
To order RAND documents or to obtain additional information, contact
Distribution Services: Telephone: (310) 451-7002;
Fax: (310) 451-6915; Email: order@rand.org

Preface

Since August 2003, the North Atlantic Treaty Organization (NATO) has had a substantial military presence in Afghanistan, culminating in operations spanning the country beginning in October 2006. For the first time in the history of the alliance, NATO is operating on territory outside of Europe and is responsible for the security of a non-member state. The risks and implications entailed in such a mission are far reaching, to say the least, and, in some ways, can be compared with other momentous challenges that NATO has confronted over its 60-year history.

This monograph evaluates NATO's role as an alliance, both with regard to its internal dynamics and its role in facing external security threats. It focuses on NATO's role in Afghanistan in particular and the implications that this undertaking and its results could have for the future of the alliance.

The document is an outgrowth of a research project, "Risks and Rewards in U.S. Alliances." The project sought to examine pressures on alliance structures, and on U.S. allies more generally, to better understand what the United States and its key partners seek to gain from such alliances; how changing security circumstances are shaping and, in some circumstances, recasting the nature of these partnerships; and, more generally, to explore the costs and benefits of sustaining alliance relationships into the future. Additionally, the project aimed to shed light on strategies that could maximize the benefits of key partnerships into the indefinite future, as well as strategies to share and distribute among allies the risks that remain in ways conducive to effectively functioning alliance relations.

The research reported here was sponsored by Headquarters United States Air Force, Directorate of Operational Plans and Joint Matters (HQ USAF/A5X) and conducted within the Strategy and Doctrine Program of RAND Project AIR FORCE.

This document should be of interest to a broad audience, from policymakers and decisionmakers to students of security studies. This monograph provides insights and recommendations for strengthening alliance structures amidst a changing and challenging security environment.

RAND Project AIR FORCE

RAND Project AIR FORCE (PAF), a division of the RAND Corporation, is the U.S. Air Force's federally funded research and development center for studies and analyses. PAF provides the Air Force with independent analyses of policy alternatives affecting the development, employment, combat readiness, and support of current and future aerospace forces. Research is conducted in four programs: Force Modernization and Employment; Manpower, Personnel, and Training; Resource Management; and Strategy and Doctrine.

Additional information about PAF is available on our website: http://www.rand.org/paf/

Contents

Figures and Tables

Summary

Sixty years after its inception, NATO finds itself at what could be a pivotal and defining moment. NATO's success in Afghanistan—or lack thereof—will have significant implications for the future of the alliance. A successful mission in Afghanistan could promote the vision of NATO as a global security alliance capable of undertaking a wide scope of operations, ranging from diplomatic engagement to peacekeeping operations and even to combat operations beyond the bounds of the treaty area. Such versatility would confirm NATO's role as the most important security alliance in existence. Alternatively, failure in Afghanistan, or even an indeterminate outcome, would portend an uncertain future for NATO. Were NATO to emerge less than victorious, it would remain to be seen what lessons the alliance would retain other than determining never to embark on a mission like this again. Indeed, it is entirely possible that NATO would conclude that nation-building in Afghanistan was not that important after all and not worth the risk, on the assumption that the real goal was to preclude al Qaeda from reestablishing a sanctuary there. While this may spare NATO the painful experience of learning hard lessons, it would not spare the pain felt for those lives lost.

The Americanization of the effort, a result of the March and December 2009 decisions by the U.S. administration to significantly increase U.S. troops and equipment, provided renewed momentum to the mission, in addition to much-needed resources. Nevertheless, while the Americanization may be good for Afghanistan, it may prove to be bad for NATO as an alliance. Indeed, absent a decision to increase their own contributions in kind, alliance partners instead find themselves junior partners. In an alliance that finds achieving consensus is central, having one partner clearly overshadow all others highlights the real limits of the transatlantic alliance.

The purpose of this document is to evaluate NATO's role as an alliance given NATO's past, but with a focus on NATO's present and an eye toward the future. In particular, we examine the risks, commitments, and obligations entailed in NATO's operations in Afghanistan and the effects this mission has on the alliance's internal dynamics. We draw on a wide range of sources to examine how NATO's role has been redefined over time. In doing so, we make certain observations:

- NATO assumed control of the International Security Assistance Force (ISAF) mission without a firm understanding of the demands, level of commitment, or level of resources such a mission would entail. In short, NATO had no strategy. (See pp. 16–24.)
- Despite rebalancing efforts, not all alliance members are sharing this mission's burdens—troop levels, funding, and equipment—equally. A few members are bearing the brunt of commitments for operations in Afghanistan. (See pp. 42–48.)
- Operations in Afghanistan have forced the alliance to confront something it has largely avoided in previous operations: the risk of casualties. On this all-important issue, the uneven distribution of the burdens and risks among ISAF members is having a corrosive effect on the cohesion of the alliance. (See pp. 48–56.)
- Given the risks and the nature of the threat in Afghanistan, managing the expectations of NATO members and their respective publics will require greater effort. Addressing the misalignment of expectations both within governments (between military and civilian elements) and between governments and their electorates would help foster greater cohesion between NATO forces deployed abroad and their counterparts at home and would aid the development of a more holistic long-term strategy for Afghanistan. (See pp. 60–67.)
- NATO members increasingly acknowledge that a successful long-term strategy in Afghanistan, especially given recent levels of vio-

lence and instability, must include a sustained commitment to training, equipping, advising, and assisting the Afghan National Security Forces; bolstering security in regions under threat from the Taliban or other criminal elements; strengthening governance at the local and national levels; and assisting development and reconstruction efforts. The membership has, however, not yet provided adequate resources for such a strategy. (See pp. 27–37.)

- Such a long-term strategy should also be coherent, comprehensive, and coordinated with other key powers and organizations, including the Afghan government, the United Nations, and the European Union. Most important, these entities need to align their strategies with the others and work toward compatible and complimentary time lines. As it stands, the American, European, and Afghan partners are all working under very different time lines—and in some instances, different goals. (See pp. 27–39 and 60–67.)
- Additionally, NATO's role in Afghanistan has opened opportunities for constructive outreach to regional powers that have a vested interest in, and influence on, the outcome of operations in Afghanistan. For example, NATO, as a forum, could be a valuable tool for a coordinated effort to reach out politically to garner more-effective support from Pakistan. (See pp. 64–65.)
- Finally, the success and survival of the alliance beyond Afghanistan will require the alliance to redefine the roles of NATO members and nonmembers, as well as its relationships with the United Nations and the European Union. (See pp. 56–60.)

The list of issues NATO faces is long and daunting and extends beyond the borders of the member countries. Yet, if the goal is indeed to look toward the future, these are issues the alliance must confront; failure to do so would risk the long-term success and sustainability of the alliance.

Acknowledgments

We thank our project sponsor, Lt Gen William Rew, and our office of primary responsibility, Headquarters United States Air Force, Directorate of Operational Plans and Joint Matters, for their support and contributions. Additionally, we would like to thank our RAND colleagues, Nora Bensahel and Paula Thornhill, for their support. We also extend our gratitude to Maj Gen Joseph Brown (U.S. Air Force), LTG Karl Eikenberry (U.S. Army, ret.), Gen. James Jones (U.S. Marine Corps, ret.), and David Ochmanek for their time and comments. In addition, we are grateful to COL Joseph Collins (U.S. Army, ret.) and Christopher Chivvis for their careful review of this report. We also thank Phyllis Gilmore for her careful editing of this document. Finally, we extend our appreciation to Colleen Geiselhart, Leslie Thornton, and Meagan Smith for their superb assistance throughout the duration of this project.

Abbreviations

ANA	Afghan National Army
ANP	Afghan National Police
ANSF	Afghan National Security Forces
EU	European Union
GDR	German Democratic Republic [East Germany]
ISAF	International Security Assistance Force
NATO	North Atlantic Treaty Organization
NRF	NATO Response Force
OEF	Operation Enduring Freedom
POMLT	police operational mentoring and liaison team
PRT	Provincial Reconstruction Team
UK	United Kingdom
UN	United Nations
UNSCR	United Nations Security Council Resolution

CHAPTER ONE

Introduction

In September 2006, as the North Atlantic Treaty Organization (NATO) was assuming overall responsibility for all military operations in Afghanistan, NATO's military commander, General James Jones, was working feverishly behind the scenes to gain support from partner nations to commit the troops and materiel he felt were necessary to succeed in the new tasks that the alliance had assigned to him. Seemingly with the stroke of a pen, NATO was taking a bold step—and taking on a host of new risks—yet it engaged in endless debates about sending even modest increments of additional troops and equipment to support what was, by any standard, a greatly expanded and extraordinarily difficult mission in Afghanistan. Just as NATO was stepping up, at least in theory, Afghanistan was showing more and more signs of falling apart. Yet, as it was stepping up, NATO lacked an overriding concept of or support for the mission itself, leaving many to wonder what would fall apart first: Afghanistan or the International Security Assistance Force (ISAF) mission.

This was not a new situation for General Jones; for his predecessor, General Joseph Ralston; for their successors, General Bantz (John) Craddock and Admiral James G. Stavridis; or for the alliance itself. Although NATO's political leadership had taken on more and more responsibilities in Afghanistan since 2002, when the alliance first became involved there after the fall of the Taliban, allied leaders never seemed willing to provide the mandate or commit the resources necessary for NATO's military commanders to succeed. Indeed, even the recent Americanization of the effort (stemming from the decisions in

March and December 2009 to significantly increase U.S. troops and equipment) carries its own risks and ramifications if NATO members choose not to follow in suit. In a sense, by involving itself in Afghanistan, NATO appears intent on demonstrating that it is still capable of doing something. Yet, in this case, the alliance does not appear to have deemed the challenge important enough to show that NATO was doing all it could. This was particularly so if doing all it could meant committing more troops and equipment and giving these forces— and the NATO commander—the authority to confront Afghanistan's most serious challenges, which, in this case, included the resurgence of Taliban forces and attacks from other extremist elements.

In a very real sense, NATO appears to have stumbled into Afghanistan with little or no debate about direction—the purpose of the mission, the resources it would need, and how it might mark a new chapter in NATO's long and storied history. Indeed, for an institution with a history of long and agonizing debates over all big (and most small) matters, NATO's role in Afghanistan came about almost as an afterthought, although one that will have profound effects for the future of the alliance. NATO's success could usher in a new era of transatlantic cooperation on a host of global issues and could pave the way for a new set of global partnerships.[1] Failure, or even a bad stumble, could lead NATO into a long period of introspection and retrenchment.[2] Members and nonmembers alike would inevitably question whether NATO is indeed able to perform successfully as a global security provider. Consequently, such a failure would result in reassessment of NATO's role and purpose and even of its continuing necessity and viability as an

---

[1] The 2006 NATO summit in Riga, Latvia, stressed the need to develop and maintain global partnerships because of "the global threats and challenges the Alliance is facing and the long-distance nature of recent NATO-led operations and missions." The same emphasis on partnerships was repeated at the Bucharest, Romania, summit over a year later. See NATO, "NATO's Partnerships," Riga Summit Guide, press kit, 2006; NATO, "Contact Countries," *Bucharest Summit Guide*, 2008.

[2] We are quick to acknowledge that success has yet to be defined, although NATO leaders have spoken of improved security, reconstruction and development, and governance at various times. See, for example, NATO, "Progress in Afghanistan: Bucharest Summit," April 2–4, 2008c.

alliance. While new security problems, such as Iran's quest for nuclear weapons, could spark a revival in the alliance, the aftershocks of failure in Afghanistan could prove debilitating. This would, after all, be the first instance in which the alliance was called into action and failed.[3] In this sense, the risks associated with NATO's foray into Afghanistan are extraordinary.

Whatever the outcome, NATO's decision to become involved in Afghanistan—at first in a very limited role but ultimately taking responsibility for the security and reconstruction of the entire state—will be remembered as a watershed event for the alliance and will be counted among the handful of fateful decisions that shaped the alliance's history.

This monograph considers NATO's future through the lens of its involvement in Afghanistan. It focuses particularly on how NATO manages risk in light of its new commitments and obligations. In Chapter Two, we begin by briefly examining the sweep of NATO's history, including the early days of the alliance; the key milestones of the Cold War; and NATO's responses to significant events, such as the fall of the Berlin Wall and the terrorist attacks of September 11, 2001. Chapters Three, Four, and Five follow NATO as it accepts its role as a security provider after 9/11, then moves into Afghanistan. These chapters consider NATO's performance before and during its commitment in Afghanistan, from the onset of its limited role to its command of ISAF and direct roles in both peacekeeping and combat operations. We thus consider the risks that NATO member states face in Afghanistan, focusing in particular on shared burdens, which now for the first time include shared casualties (who dies for the alliance); redefining roles and responsibilities in the alliance (who among NATO and non-NATO countries is capable of doing what); and managing expectations among NATO's leaders and supporting publics, particularly as missions become both long and demanding. Chapter Six concludes with a

---

[3] In a review of this monograph, Colonel (ret.) Joseph Collins observed that, although the NATO operation in Kosovo was a technical success mainly because of U.S. airpower, it was less of a success for the NATO alliance and a preview of challenges NATO would face in Afghanistan.

discussion of the future of NATO and how its role in Afghanistan will affect NATO's role as a global security provider in the years to come.

CHAPTER TWO

The NATO That Once Was

NATO was not part of the initial post–World War II design. Initial planning for the postwar order focused on the creation of global entities—the United Nations (UN), the International Monetary Fund, and the World Bank—and enforcement by the "Four Policemen": the United States, Great Britain, the Soviet Union, and China.[1] Several key elements of this plan did not survive Roosevelt's death in 1945; some parts did not survive the decade; and still other parts, rather amazingly, survive to this day.

NATO was born of necessity as postwar euphoria gave way to ever-increasing tensions with the Soviet Union in Europe and with Northeast Asia. Communist success in China and China's open, although short-lived, embrace of Moscow only fueled the need for action. Plans for global security arrangements, created during the middle to waning days of World War II, gave way to two distinct camps: East and West. NATO would become the centerpiece of security cooperation for the West.[2]

But the all-too-apparent need for NATO did not mean that creating the alliance would be simple or seamless. At the heart of the debate was deep-seated concern over what role defeated and occupied Germany should play in the new alliance. France, in particular, was at the center of the debate.

---

[1] John Lewis Gaddis, *Strategies of Containment: A Critical Appraisal of Postwar American National Security*, New York: Oxford University Press, 1982, p. 10.

[2] Of historical note, plans for a North Atlantic Treaty came from the Europeans themselves (Gaddis, 1982, p. 72).

Although most understood that the Federal Republic of Germany needed to be anchored in a new transatlantic relationship, there was genuine concern about Germany's military role in the alliance. Many observers thought that Germany should be relegated to a passive recipient of security that would be provided by the victorious allies. Many harbored deep anxieties about German rearmament.[3]

Given demonstrable Soviet expansionist designs and growing Soviet and Warsaw Pact military capabilities, the question of risks and rewards in the newly formed alliance seemed relatively straightforward: In exchange for acknowledgment of U.S. leadership and for the allies' contributions to the common defense, the United States was prepared to demonstrate its share in Western Europe's security risks by committing itself militarily to the defense of NATO Europe. That commitment included the potential use of U.S. and, later, NATO-controlled nuclear weapons. In essence, NATO's European partners acceded to becoming importers of security, with the United States becoming the predominant exporter. Over time, however, the United States wanted more than a leadership role for its contributions. It also expected NATO's European members to be active, not passive, contributors to Europe's defense. Year after year, decade after decade, American leaders would lament that, although risks were being shared, as had been conceived in the earliest days of the alliance, the burdens (of making good on commitments) were not. As the European NATO states emerged from their immediate postwar destruction, becoming prosperous, thriving economies, the chorus of these American concerns grew louder. That chorus continued through the final days of the Cold War.[4]

---

[3] For more on the rearmament debate and France's concerns in particular, see "Sound and Fury: The Debate over German Rearmament," Ch. 5 in William I. Hitchcock, *France Restored: Cold War Diplomacy and the Quest for Leadership in Europe, 1944–1954*, Chapel Hill, N.C.: University of North Carolina Press, 1998, pp. 133–168. See also Dean Acheson, *Present at the Creation*, New York: Norton and Company, 1969, pp. 608–609.

[4] In the earliest days of the alliance, Washington was concerned that NATO Europe would sacrifice economic reconstruction for military preparedness. By the mid-1960s, these concerns would abate, and new concerns would arise about Europe's "insufficient" contributions to North Atlantic security. See, for example, Earl C. Ravenal, "Europe Without America: The Erosion of NATO," *Foreign Affairs*, Vol. 63, No. 5, Summer 1985.

And the United States wanted more. The United States also expected broader political support for its varying agendas beyond Europe. The United States maintained strong pressure on selected NATO partners to decolonize.[5] It opposed certain British and French roles in the Middle East; sought support for U.S. military involvement in Southeast Asia; and, later, tried to solicit support for U.S. policies in the Middle East.

Nuclear weapons would remain a central and enormously sensitive topic. Although American and European leaders alike understood and accepted the rationale for relying on nuclear weapons and a tangible threat of escalation to compensate for a perceived conventional inferiority, they were also wary about the role nuclear weapons might play in an actual crisis or war. When Charles DeGaulle purportedly asked whether "any U.S. President is prepared to sacrifice New York to save Paris,"[6] he gave voice to broader European anxieties about the risks the United States might be willing to take on behalf of its European partners but presented only half the debate. The other half seized on what it saw as the distinct possibility that Washington might actually be willing to use nuclear weapons in a European war, might actually be willing "to fight to the last European"—to avoid risking the U.S. mainland.[7] The argument ran that Washington might be willing to incur great risks to protect its allies, but its foremost priority was to protect the population of the United States. One had to presume Washington would not shrink from any option available to do so. This tension was managed throughout the Cold War years but never resolved.

Still, throughout the Cold War, the United States never allowed policy differences with its European partners, including France, to overshadow its abiding interests in containing Soviet influence and deterring Soviet military threats to Europe. Washington's European partners, for their part, found ways to achieve a workable balance between being led by the United States and being treated as equal partners.

---

5 This policy, of course, predated the establishment of NATO.

6 "The Frustrated West," *Time*, May 19, 1961.

7 Roger Cohen, "Over There; Why the Yanks Are Going. Yet Again," *New York Times*, November 26, 1995.

Although NATO seemed to be in perpetual crisis,[8] its crises focused almost entirely on how to achieve lasting security in Europe, not on whether security was worth achieving.

The fall of the Berlin Wall, the collapse of the Warsaw Pact, and the disintegration of the Soviet Union created a degree of euphoria in Europe perhaps never before experienced in its long and turbulent history. These events also raised questions about the future of the alliance that had been so successful in bringing about the circumstances that seemed more a dream than reality. German unification would be the first test.

Much like the debate over Germany's role in NATO and German rearmament, the idea of German unification generated trepidation in many circles, not just in Moscow, but also in Paris and London. If the expressed purpose for NATO was to protect members against Soviet aggression, an implicit role was to link Germany inextricably to its Western partners to preclude repetition of the two calamitous wars of the 20th century. As Lord Ismay, NATO's first Secretary General, reportedly stated, NATO's purpose was to "keep the Americans in, the Russians out and the Germans down."[9] Those opposing rapid German unification did so largely on the grounds that a united Germany had much more potential to become an independent Germany, capable of separating from its NATO partners. Those arguing in favor of rapid unification maintained that a united Germany would be linked to the West not only through NATO but, more importantly, through the European Community (soon to become the European Union [EU]).[10] At the same time, internal instability in the German Democratic Republic (GDR) was steadily increasing and threatening to tear the country apart. As a result, Helmut Kohl's government viewed unifica-

---

[8]   See, for example, Henry A. Kissinger, *The Troubled Partnership: A Re-Appraisal of the Atlantic Alliance*, New York: McGraw-Hill, 1965.

[9]   Andrés Ortega and Tomas Valasek, "Debate: Are the Challenges NATO Faces Today as Great as They Were in the Cold War?" *NATO Review*, Winter 2003.

[10]   See, for example, Philip D. Zelikow and Condoleezza Rice, *Germany Unified and Europe Transformed: A Study in Statecraft*, Cambridge, Mass.: Harvard University Press, 1997, pp. 157–160.

tion with the Federal Republic of Germany as a better approach than attempting to reform and democratize the GDR.[11] Concerns about the stability of East Germany trumped the broader debate over the implications of a unified Germany; consequently, unification proceeded quickly, and the GDR's fate was settled within a year.[12]

With the German question settled—or least muted for the time being—attention turned rapidly to the issue of NATO's identity and purpose after the Cold War.[13] With Central and Eastern Europe untethered and the Balkans simmering, many began arguing for a broadened NATO role. The tagline "out of area or out of business" expressed a school of thought that held that NATO needed to embrace Central and Eastern Europe and help bring stability to the Balkans lest it face bankruptcy as an institution.[14] According to this view, it was vital that NATO demonstrate its relevance to the most pressing security issues Europe faced. Were it not up to the task of extending stability, NATO would not long survive.

Looking back now, after three post–Cold War rounds of NATO enlargement and two reasonably successful interventions in the Balkans, expanding NATO's reach to the periphery of Europe seems natural and inevitable, even though each initiative prompted opposition from Moscow. But the decision to enlarge NATO in the first place was a close call, with debate circling largely around potential risks. Those

---

[11] In hindsight, it is now clear that Helmut Kohl was the driving force behind the West German position. See Zelikow and Rice, 1997.

[12] Zelikow and Rice, 1997.

[13] As an attempt to revitalize NATO's purpose, the alliance agreed on and publicly released the new Strategic Concept at the NATO meeting in Rome in November 1991 (previous versions were classified). The concept took into account the changing security environment, German unification, ongoing transformation in the former Soviet Union, and arms control issues. It restated the purpose of NATO and laid out the fundamental tasks of the alliance. Similarly, in 1999, the Strategic Concept was updated to describe a NATO that was more flexible and able to conduct new missions outside its members' territories, such as in Kosovo and Bosnia, and that was larger and prepared to address such new security threats as weapons of mass destruction and terrorism. See NATO, "Strategic Concept," web page, last updated July 31, 2010f.

[14] See Ronald D. Asmus, *Opening NATO's Door*, New York: Columbia University Press, 2002.

opposed to enlargement questioned what NATO was taking on, both in terms of cost and mission.[15] Those opposed to intervention in the Balkans raised their objections largely on the basis that, once NATO was involved, it would never be able to extricate itself. Opponents, in particular, were quick to raise Bismarck's famous quip that the Balkans were "not worth the bones of a Pomeranian grenadier."[16]

The Kosovo experience, in particular, produced deep divisions inside NATO—and in the U.S. administration—because NATO was being committed not merely to enforce a peace settlement but to create conditions for change through the coercive use of force.[17] As the bombing of Serbia and Serbian forces in Kosovo continued from days to weeks to months,[18] several of NATO's now 19 members grew increasingly uneasy about the mission the alliance had adopted and the possible outcomes. Serbian leader Slobodan Milosevic finally did capitulate after 79 days of bombing, but the alliance itself had been shaken greatly by the experience. An implicit lesson for many in the United

---

[15] As the debate on NATO membership for the Czech Republic, Hungary, and Poland unfolded, one question was whether it would simply cost these nations less to join NATO than to develop their own defenses individually. Similarly, NATO members also asked how much it would cost NATO to bring the candidate nations' defenses up to alliance standards. Several members were concerned about NATO's overall mission and whether enlargement was a move in the right direction. Those against enlargement argued that NATO did not face a threat that warranted enlargement, which would in turn only aggravate relations with Russia and create more problems than solutions. Despite these concerns, in the end, consensus emerged that it would be in NATO's interests to accept candidates into the alliance that met the stated requirements for NATO membership because the benefits of their membership would outweigh the costs. See Linda D. Kozaryn, "'Mr. NATO' Explains Enlargement," American Forces Press Service, April 1998.

[16] See, for example, François de Rose, "A Future Perspective for the Alliance," *NATO Review*, Vol. 43, No. 4, July 1995.

[17] See Daniel L. Byman, Matthew C. Waxman, and Eric Larson, *Air Power as a Coercive Instrument*, Santa Monica, Calif.: RAND Corporation, MR-1061-AF, 1999, and Stephen T. Hosmer, *The Conflict Over Kosovo: Why Milosevic Decided to Settle When He Did*, Santa Monica, Calif.: RAND Corporation, MR-1351-AF, 2001.

[18] Then–NATO commander General Wesley Clark, along other allied leaders, assumed Serbian leaders would capitulate within three days. For further discussion, see Hosmer, 2001, pp. 17–18.

States and Europe was that, when it came to the coercive use of force, NATO would not be up to the task again anytime soon.[19]

---

[19] See, for example, Benjamin S. Lambeth, "Lessons from the War in Kosovo," *Joint Force Quarterly*, Vol. 30, Spring 2002; Daniel L. Byman and Matthew C. Waxman, "Kosovo and the Great Air Power Debate," *International Security*, Vol. 24, No. 4, Spring 2000; and Bruce R. Nardulli, Walter L. Perry, Bruce Pirnie, John Gordon IV, and John G. McGinn, *Disjointed War: Military Operations in Kosovo, 1999*, Santa Monica, Calif.: RAND Corporation, MR-1406-A, 2002.

CHAPTER THREE

Redefining NATO's Role: 9/11 to Afghanistan

The September 2001 terrorist attacks on the United States provided a
new watershed for NATO. Americans and Europeans alike were deeply
shocked and shaken by the attacks,[1] and the U.S. government and
international community felt an impetus for an immediate response.
In a strong showing of support to the United States and at the urging
of NATO Secretary General George Robertson, the North Atlantic
Council made an unprecedented decision on September 12, 2001, to
invoke Article V of the NATO charter, which states that an attack on
one NATO member was an attack on all NATO members. Shortly
thereafter, NATO submitted a proposal to the United States listing
a set of possible military functions it could provide to assist with the
fight against terrorism in Afghanistan.[2] However, deep differences
remained among NATO members about appropriate courses of action
and the role of the alliance in meeting broader security challenges.
Although it had not specifically requested the Article V declaration, the
United States was eager to accept allied contributions, but not at the
cost of delaying action or compromising its ultimate goal of destroying
al Qaeda's stronghold, capturing its leaders, and ending Taliban rule in
Afghanistan. As a result, the United States ultimately declined the offer
of direct support from NATO. Instead, with the help of a few NATO

---

[1] See Jean-Marie Colombani, "Nous Sommes Tous Américains [We Are All Americans],"
Le Monde, September 12, 2001.

[2] Gerard Baker, "NATO Is Not Dead but Missing in Action," *Financial Times*, November
21, 2002.

partner countries,[3] the United States began preparations for large-scale operations in Afghanistan: Operation Enduring Freedom (OEF), led by U.S. armed forces, would begin on October 7, 2001.

In late September 2001, in the run-up to OEF, U.S. Secretary of Defense Donald Rumsfeld tried to address the nature of the military challenges—as he saw them—in an attempt to define the new "war on terrorism" and how military operations needed to adapt to it. Rumsfeld stated, "the mission will define the coalition—not the other way around."[4] Many viewed this as a slap at NATO and a rejection of the way NATO had operated over its history. Rumsfeld's position, as well as Washington's "you're with us or against us" attitude,[5] made many in Europe express skepticism about the longer-term future of the alliance.[6] To many, U.S. reluctance to work with the alliance—even after the first-ever invocation of Article V—had a damaging effect on NATO, making it seem less viable and certainly less important.[7] As NATO Secretary General George Robertson would later admit, the U.S. decision to ignore the alliance "left some bruises behind."[8]

Although they were no less appalled by the 9/11 attacks than American leaders, several European leaders continued to voice caution

---

[3] For further discussion of European contributions, as well as NATO's indirect support, see Nora Bensahel, *The Counterterror Coalitions: Cooperation with Europe, NATO, and the European Union*, Santa Monica, Calif.: RAND Corporation, MR-1746-AF, 2003.

[4] Secretary of Defense Donald H. Rumsfeld, "A New Kind of War," *New York Times*, September 27, 2001.

[5] President George W. Bush, "Address to a Joint Session of Congress and the American People," Washington, D.C.: The White House, Office of the Press Secretary, September 20, 2001.

[6] See, for example, Steven Erlanger, "For NATO, Little Is Sure Now but Growth," *New York Times*, May 19, 2002. Indeed, one commentator of this monograph noted that, in retrospect, the challenges NATO has faced since assuming the entire mission in late 2006 and the subsequent re-Americanization of the effort in 2008 could be seen to confirm U.S. hesitance to work with the alliance at the onset.

[7] Judy Dempsey, "If Bush Does Not Make Clear that NATO Can Be Involved in Critical Issues, the Alliance Will Atrophy," *Financial Times*, November 20, 2002b.

[8] Robert G. Kaiser and Keith B. Richburg, "NATO Looking Ahead to a Mission Makeover," *Washington Post*, November 5, 2002.

over America's all-out "war on terror" over the following year,[9] asking aloud whether such a direct and frontal approach (the idea that the best defense had to be a good offense[10]) would achieve the desired results. Many in Europe, including several of the Bush administration's close partners in the United Kingdom (UK), took the position that Europeans had long lived with the threat of terrorism and had learned to contain the threat without confronting the need to go to war. These voices respected Washington's goal of ending al Qaeda's sanctuary in Afghanistan and even ending the Taliban regime's rule there, but they were deeply concerned about where Washington's new assertiveness would take it, and them, next. In short, they were concerned about whether the risks associated with aligning with Washington in its war on terror outweighed the rewards, particularly if Washington was heading into destinations unknown or perhaps too well known, such as Iraq.

This is not to suggest that European leaders were, or are, of a single mind on the issue. Donald Rumsfeld's quip about "old Europe and new Europe" resonated with many on both sides of the Atlantic.[11] It did so not so much because Rumsfeld accurately captured the cleavages in European opinion but because he recognized that European leaders had widely different views on the importance of divergent security threats to Europe and NATO, and that France and Germany, in particular, did not speak for all of Europe. Rumsfeld's now-famous words helped to spark a period of introspection in Europe about security matters in general, the various paths the United States and its European partners were following, and the future of the NATO alliance. The

---

[9] See Robert Graham and Haig Simonian, "Chirac Cautions Washington Against Unilateral Use of Force," *Financial Times*, August 30, 2002; Charles M. Sennott, "Nations Mark Sept. 11 with Mixed Feelings: Much Support, But Some Fault US Policy Course," *Boston Globe*, September 12, 2002; Glenn Kessler, "Diplomatic Gap Between U.S., Its Allies Widens," *Washington Post*, September 1, 2002.

[10] Secretary of Defense Donald H. Rumsfeld, "'21st Century Transformation' of U.S. Armed Forces," remarks, National Defense University, Fort McNair, Washington, D.C., January 31, 2002.

[11] Donald H. Rumsfeld, with Richard B. Myers, "Secretary Rumsfeld Briefs at Foreign Press Center," transcript, January 22, 2003.

unveiling of the Bush administration's views on "preemption" and the debate over war in Iraq brought these matters into stark relief.

Ultimately, the U.S. decision in fall 2001 to undertake the war in Afghanistan with only indirect NATO support was largely an effort to avoid the constraints that a coalition might impose. If the United States military and its partners were indeed set to face a new set of security challenges that required a flexible and adaptable force, some feared coalition constraints would hamper efforts to achieve the desired objectives swiftly and decisively. As a result, to achieve its objectives in Afghanistan and maintain total operational control, the United States would pursue "a coalition of committed countries, if possible, but acting alone if necessary."[12] This decision further perpetuated NATO's struggle to prove its relevance and define its role in the post–9/11 world. While NATO as a whole understood the threat of terrorism and recognized the need for action to address it, it lacked consensus on what kind of action that should be. The impetus to act could not be ignored.

An Opportunity for NATO in Afghanistan?

The objective for U.S. forces in OEF was to "disrupt the use of Afghanistan as a terrorist base of operations, and to attack the military capability of the Taliban regime."[13] The United States was able to achieve military victory relatively quickly following the start of operations in October 2001, thanks in part to substantial support from several countries, including special operations forces from Canada, Denmark, Norway, and Germany; land forces, aircraft, and a carrier battle group from France; and significant military and diplomatic support from the UK.[14] The quick success U.S. forces achieved in OEF resulted in

---

[12] Bob Woodward, *Plan of Attack*, New York: Simon and Schuster, 2004, p. 155.

[13] George W. Bush, "Presidential Address to the Nation," transcript, Washington, D.C.: The White House, Office of the Press Secretary, October 7, 2001.

[14] For more contributions, see U.S. Department of State, Bureau of European and Eurasian Affairs, "NATO: Coalition Contributions to the War on Terrorism," fact sheet, Washington, D.C., October 24, 2002.

the UN-supported Bonn Peace Agreement (signed December 5, 2001, at the Bonn conference in Germany), which established an interim Afghan government, the Afghan Transitional Authority, on December 22, 2001, in addition to a UN-mandated international force to provide security throughout the transition process.[15] The international security force—officially named ISAF—was specifically mandated to support the Afghan Transitional Authority "in the maintenance of security in Kabul and its surrounding areas, so that the Afghan Interim Authority as well as the personnel of the United Nations can operate in a secure environment."[16] UN member countries volunteered at six-month intervals to lead the ISAF mission: The UK was the first to lead ISAF, designating Major General John McColl as commander.[17]

But because of the short rotation, the British had no sooner accepted command than they were already planning for their successors. In the summer of 2002, ISAF leadership was transferred to Turkey, and the question was soon raised whether transferring power every six months would ultimately become counterproductive. Since many of the countries participating in the ISAF mission were also NATO members, the idea quietly but rather quickly spread that perhaps NATO, as an organization, could play a greater role in the ISAF mission. In June 2002, Secretary General George Robertson seemingly dispelled rumors that NATO would seek a more active "out of area" role by stating that NATO is "a defence Alliance, we remain a defence Alliance, we do not go out looking for problems to solve."[18]

---

[15] For the full text of the agreement, see Agreement on Provisional Arrangements in Afghanistan Pending the Re-Establishment of Permanent Government Institutions, Bonn, Germany, December 5, 2001. See also UNSCR 1386, on Afghanistan and the International Security Force, New York, December 20, 2001.

[16] UNSCR 1386, 2001. For more background, see James L. Jones, "NATO's Role in Afghanistan," transcript of presentation to Council on Foreign Relations, October 4, 2006a.

[17] Note that while ISAF was being established, U.S. forces continued to conduct operations throughout Afghanistan. By containing ISAF's presence to Kabul and the immediate vicinity, this enabled U.S. forces to continue military operations throughout the rest of Afghanistan with minimal operational constraints.

[18] Lord George Robertson, NATO Secretary General, transcript of press conference, Brussels: NATO Headquarters, June 6, 2002.

However, less than three months later, in September 2002, Robertson emphasized the need to refocus NATO's military capabilities on 21st-century threats, including terrorism and the dangers of weapons of mass destruction, "to root them out and destroy them."[19]

Germany and the Netherlands were poised to take control of ISAF from Turkey in early 2003. Yet the demands of the mission, coupled with operational limitations, were becoming increasingly evident. In October 2002, Germany and the Netherlands jointly asked NATO's North Atlantic Council for its support for the ISAF mission once the two nations assumed command.[20] The letter specifically requested that NATO provide "planning, strategic airlift, logistics, communication and intelligence support" to ISAF troops in Kabul, Afghanistan.[21] NATO agreed on October 17, 2002.[22] However, not all NATO members supported the idea of NATO expanding its role in Afghanistan when Germany proposed the idea in early 2003 (see Chapter Four). The government of France, in particular, voiced significant concerns. In April 2003, France subsequently dropped its objections to NATO's expanded role in Afghanistan, largely as an attempt to repair fractures in the alliance resulting from its vocal objection to a NATO role in Iraq (discussed in the next subsection).[23] As Chapter Four will discuss further, the NATO heads of state reached a consensus in early 2003

---

[19] Gerry J. Gilmore, "NATO Must Plan for Future Role, Robertson Tells Ministers," American Forces Press Service, September 24, 2002. Lord George Robertson, NATO Secretary General, "Opening Statement," Informal Meeting of the North Atlantic Council at the Level of Defence Ministers," Warsaw, Poland, September 21, 2002.

[20] NATO, "NATO to Support ISAF 3," *NATO Update*, November 27, 2002. See also Klaus Naumann, "Security Without the United States? Europe's Perception of NATO," *Strategic Studies Quarterly*, Fall 2009, p. 59.

[21] Ian Black, "NATO Emerges from Bunker with New Role in Afghanistan," *The Guardian*, November 15, 2002, and Judy Dempsey, "NATO Poised to Take Role in Kabul Security," *Financial Times*, November 12, 2002a.

[22] NATO, 2002.

[23] Karen DeYoung, "Chirac Moves to Repair U.S. Ties; Relations Still Strained Despite French Overtures," *Washington Post*, April 16, 2003; Judy Dempsey, "New NATO Force to Be Launched in October: Commander Sees the Need for 'A Vehicle for the Transformation of the Military Alliance,'" *Financial Times*, April 25, 2003.

that NATO should assume greater responsibilities in Afghanistan and that a role for NATO in Afghanistan would help strengthen the alliance.

Afghanistan to Iraq: Where Does NATO Fit In?

Shortly after the NATO decision to assist Germany's and the Netherlands' command of the ISAF mission in Afghanistan, the NATO heads of state met in Prague. The Prague summit in November 2002 will ultimately be remembered for the decision to invite seven new members into the alliance,[24] but it also provided a venue for the United States to repair divisions in the alliance by reconfirming its own commitment to NATO, as well as a chance to propose a role for NATO in U.S.-led operations in Iraq.

The addition of seven new members (often referred to as the "big bang" enlargement) to NATO further confirmed that the alliance was changing. On one hand, this enlargement was an opportunity for NATO members to reaffirm their commitments to the transatlantic alliance as an organization ready and willing to confront future security challenges. On the other hand, this move led some to fear that such sudden and significant growth would render NATO irrelevant and that it would be all but impossible for 26 members to act as a cohesive and unified group.[25] Nevertheless, despite such uncertainties, the NATO heads of state were willing to accept the risks of enlargement and now faced the decision of what mission NATO should take on next.

For the United States, operations in Afghanistan and concerns over Iraq led to the recognition that, in the long term, a stable, permanent NATO alliance would enhance U.S. security and that a con-

---

[24] The seven new members were Bulgaria, Estonia, Latvia, Lithuania, Romania, Slovakia, and Slovenia.

[25] Critics often mused that, if NATO decisions were hard to achieve with 16 or 19 members, consider the difficulty of reaching consensus with 26 members. However, others noted that, in terms of reaching a consensus, the number of members matters less than their availability and willingness to cooperate.

certed effort should be made to maintain and strengthen NATO, including enhanced military capabilities. In September 2002, as part of this recommitment to NATO, the United States proposed the development of a NATO Response Force (NRF)—a force of up to 25,000 troops with a wide range of capabilities and the ability to mobilize and deploy to target zones in a few weeks' time—as well as a subsequent shift in the NATO military command structure.[26] To meet these dual objectives, the United States argued for a new organizational structure through which countries could provide niche capabilities in areas of particular specialty, rather than pushing for proportional contributions.[27] With NATO continuing to enlarge and accept new members, such a refocused strategy would enable smaller countries to contribute tailored capabilities to NATO's overall military strength, rather than feel pressured to invest more of their limited resources in areas where NATO already had ample strength, such as general-purpose ground forces or fighter aircraft.

To some NATO allies, the NRF proposal was welcome, viewed as a leverage point against U.S. unilateralism and "a sign that Washington does not want to downgrade NATO to a mere political club that threatens eventually to alienate its European allies."[28] Other Europeans, however, were concerned, fearing that the NRF would become a tool for U.S. foreign policy. Some of the same Europeans were also trying to harmonize EU efforts to create its own rapid-reaction force. For example, French President Jacques Chirac was emphatic in arguing

---

[26] Note that the 25,000 troops include land, air, and sea forces. This can include a brigade-size land component, a naval task force, an amphibious task group, an air component, and special forces. For more information, see NATO, "The NATO Response Force: At the Centre of NATO Transformation," web page, updated June 10, 2010d.

[27] George W. Bush, "President Bush Previews Historic NATO Summit in Prague Speech: Remarks by the President to Prague Atlantic Student Summit," Prague, Czech Republic, November 20, 2002. As an example of niche capabilities, many analysts pointed to the Czech Republic's ability to detect the presence of nuclear, biological, and chemical weapons on the battlefield, a capability in short supply in NATO and one with which the Czechs had achieved particular proficiency.

[28] Dempsey, 2002b.

that NATO's plans not conflict with, or preclude, EU plans.[29] Nevertheless, the alliance soon agreed to endorse and support the creation of the NRF. The NRF would consist entirely of European military forces and would not conflict with the EU's plans to create its own rapid-reaction force.[30]

NATO's decision to create the NRF occurred as the United States debated using force to bring down Saddam Hussein's regime. When the debate shifted to what forces could be brought to bear in the event of an attack, the NRF was suggested as one potential contribution. While NATO eventually agreed to create the NRF, the alliance remained split not only on whether the NRF should be considered for Iraq but also on whether NATO should be involved in Iraq at all.[31]

While some supported the idea of NATO involvement in Iraq as a means of reconfirming its purpose as an alliance and addressing challenges in the new threat environment, others were decidedly more cautious. The skeptics saw a need to take the offensive against al Qaeda but strongly disagreed with the U.S. decision to go to war in Iraq. France and Germany, which were most vocal in opposing the war, maintained that Iraq was not a safe haven for terrorists, that the existing policy of containing Iraq was working, and that, if weapons of mass destruction existed, inspectors should be given the opportunity and sufficient time to locate them. France and Germany cautioned against what many perceived to be a U.S. rush to action, refusing to support U.S. operations in Iraq and arguing that any operation needed a UN mandate.[32] In addition, France went so far as to state it would consider vetoing a UN decision if it remained unconvinced that military action in Iraq was the

---

[29] Ian Mather, "West Outgrows NATO Paper Tiger," *The Scotsman*, November 24, 2002.

[30] In fact, the EU even enlisted NATO's assistance in the creation of this rapid-reaction force. See Joseph Fitchett, "NATO Agrees to Help New EU Force," *International Herald Tribune*, December 16, 2002.

[31] Keith B. Richburg, "NATO Blocked on Iraq Decision; France, Germany Lead Opposition to War," *Washington Post*, January 23, 2003; Thomas E. Ricks, "NATO Allies Trade Barbs Over Iraq; Rumsfeld: Critics Are Undermining Alliance's Strength," *Washington Post*, February 9, 2003.

[32] It is important to note, however, that Germany did not interfere with the deployment to Iraq of U.S. military forces stationed on, or transiting through, German territory.

best option available. Furthermore, France and Germany argued that U.S.-led action, without their support, would ultimately undermine the alliance. As French Defense Minister Michele Alliot-Marie noted, "ad hoc coalitions," or coalitions of the willing, would not be able to replace NATO and would threaten NATO's effectiveness.[33]

The debate became quite personal in tone and character. Jacques Chirac and Gerhard Schroeder strongly believed that war in Iraq would increase danger levels, not reduce them, and that the outcomes would be highly unpredictable. Neither Chirac nor Schroeder accepted the argument that promoting democracy through military occupation was the answer to the threat of jihadist-inspired terrorism, although both seemed to recognize that the status quo in the Middle East was highly fragile and perhaps untenable.[34] Indeed, both feared the spread of chaos into their own societies, which later became a reality for Chirac, although for reasons unrelated to al Qaeda. Both argued that more good could be accomplished by advancing Arab-Israeli peace, although neither had a positive agenda to put forth and neither was a particularly trusted party in the region. Most noteworthy, from the standpoint of transatlantic relations, both were prepared to accept fractures in the alliance—not just with the United States but also among Europeans—rather than support the U.S. position on Iraq.

In the case of the French government, a separate issue also remained that predated 9/11 and would continue to be a distinct source of tension with the United States. In his role as the "spokesman for Europe," Chirac had devoted most of his tenure to trying to forge a separate European identity that would occasionally complement, although more routinely balance, American security policy, be

---

[33] Ricks, 2003. Note also that "coalition of the willing" refers to the phrase then–U.S. President Bush coined in a November 2002 statement on disarming Iraq. See George W. Bush, "President Discusses Homeland Security, Economy with Cabinet," Washington, D.C.: Office of the Press Secretary, November 13, 2002.

[34] Erwan Jourand, "Chirac Backs War on Terrorism 'Without Mercy' at Francophone Summit," Agence France Presse, October 19, 2002; Elaine Sciolino, "Trans-Atlantic Disputes Over Iraq Weigh Heavily on Europeans," *New York Times*, April 2, 2003.

it on issues in Europe, the Middle East, or farther afield in Asia.[35] Others in France were much more openly suspicious of unchallenged U.S. power in the post–Cold War era. Hubert Védrine, former Minister of Foreign Affairs under Prime Minister Lionel Jospin, coined the term hyperpower in 1999 to describe, in his terms, U.S. "dominance of attitudes, concepts, language, and modes of life." It was Védrine who also asked, "How do you counterbalance these tendencies when they are abusive?"[36]

The war in Iraq would become a watershed for the United States, Europe, and NATO. Throughout its history and many crises—most of which were crises of conscience—most observers assumed that, despite hand-wringing and debate, despite name-calling and "op-ed" diplomacy, despite sometimes genuine differences over policy and strategy, when it came time for action, NATO would act as one. With France and Germany fundamentally opposed to the war, there would be no chance for NATO to act as one in Iraq. Even more than in Afghanistan, new arrangements had to be created for selected European governments to join the United States in war against Iraq; hence, a new "coalition of the willing" was born.[37] As this particular coalition of the willing came to life, many wondered whether NATO would be left on its deathbed with little hope of resuscitation. Certainly, NATO as a

---

[35] Charles Bremner, "Paris and Berlin Prepare Alliance to Rival NATO," *The Times* (London), April 28, 2003; Alan Riding, "Threats and Responses: The Europeans; With Iraq Stance, Chirac Strives for Relevance," *New York Times*, February 23, 2003. See also "US Still Bitter Over France's Opposition to Iraq War: Bush Aide," Agence France Presse, May 31, 2003; Patrick Jarreau, "America Cannot Understand Being Regarded as 'More Dangerous Than Saddam Husayn': National Security Adviser Condoleezza Rice Harks Back to Disagreement Over Iraq," *Le Monde*, June 1, 2003.

[36] "To Paris, U.S. Looks Like a Hyperpower," *International Herald Tribune*, February 5, 1999.

[37] Although originally coined to enable NATO partners to contribute to missions in a manner deemed to be politically feasible, "coalitions of the willing" took on a different, more-fractious meaning as the United States, Great Britain, Spain, Italy, Poland, and others prepared for war in Iraq. See Nora Bensahel, "Separable But Not Separate Forces: NATO's Development of the Combined Joint Task Force," *European Security*, Vol. 8, No. 2, Summer 1999.

political forum would survive, but would NATO as a military alliance survive the war in Iraq?

Turkey became a particular complication in the debate over Iraq. Turkey, fearing that war in Iraq might bring upheaval, if not war, to its own soil, wanted to enlist NATO support to protect Turkish territory but not to invade Iraq. However, Germany, France, and Belgium blocked Turkey's request, which then prompted the issue to be raised before NATO's Defense Planning Committee—in which France does not participate—to sidestep French objections. The 18 members of the committee agreed to permit NATO to deploy defensive capabilities to Turkey.[38] The debate over Turkey became emblematic of the fractures in the alliance that were hampering efforts to reach consensus on any NATO action. Secretary General Robertson was open about his concerns and fears about the future of NATO, admitting "he had written a letter to NATO heads of state warning them that the credibility of the alliance was at risk."[39]

---

[38] Vernon Loeb, "U.S. Urges NATO to Expand Role in Afghanistan," *Washington Post*, February 21, 2003. Note also that the seven recently invited members had not yet joined the alliance.

[39] Michael R. Gordon, "NATO Chief Says Alliance Needs Role in Afghanistan," *New York Times*, February 21, 2003.

CHAPTER FOUR

A Greater Role for NATO in Afghanistan

> Unlike other wars, Afghan wars become serious only when they are over.
>
> *—Sir Olaf Caroe, 1962*[1]

The debate over Iraq failed to produce a direct role for NATO. However, while the Iraq debate was under way, NATO was slowly and quietly increasing its role in Afghanistan in support of the UN-mandated ISAF mission. As NATO's presence in Afghanistan gradually increased, Germany proposed in February 2003 that NATO take over command of the ISAF mission. German Defense Minister Peter Struck met with Afghan President Hamid Karzai in Kabul to discuss the proposal. At roughly the same time, NATO's Secretary General, George Robertson, commented that NATO was "examining taking command of the peacekeepers in Afghanistan chiefly to avoid the disruption of the current system, in which command turns over every six months."[2] Embedded in the discussions was a proposal to expand the overall ISAF mission to areas outside Kabul, which was one of the stated goals of Karzai's interim government.[3]

---

[1] Sir Caroe was the last British governor on the northwest frontier province. See Olaf Caroe, *The Pathans 550 B.C.–A.D. 1957*, London: Macmillan, 1962.

[2] Keith B. Richburg, "NATO Quietly Slips into Afghan Mission; First Step Beyond Traditional Bounds," *Washington Post,* December 12, 2002.

[3] Philip Shishkin, "France Wary of Expanding NATO Peacekeeper Role; Involvement in Afghanistan Raises Concerns Over Mission of Alliance," *San Diego Union-Tribune,* February 27, 2003.

The proposal to expand NATO's role in Afghanistan met some resistance inside NATO.[4] Some member nations wondered why NATO was expanding its role and reach into Asia and asked whether NATO could succeed at such a demanding out-of-area mission. The French government explicitly stated that it was hesitant to endorse a role for NATO in Afghanistan, even if only as part of a peacekeeping mission.[5] Others were concerned about whether NATO had enough troops available to undertake the mission and whether NATO possessed sufficient lift capabilities to transport and sustain the necessary number of troops from their various countries to Afghanistan. To address these concerns, the alliance planned to reduce the size of its contingent in Bosnia, which would increase the number of NATO forces available for deployment to Afghanistan. Finally, as part of the NRF effort, NATO was taking steps to invest in new equipment and upgrade current equipment to meet the needs of equipping, deploying, and sustaining a sizeable force.

Other members supported NATO taking command of the ISAF mission. Some viewed an expanded role as a possible precursor to a postconflict role for NATO in Iraq and a suitable test of NATO's capability of succeeding in such a role.[6] Those supporting the arguments noted that the Afghan people, not just the government, welcomed an expanded role.[7] And they could point to UN support as well, particularly that of Secretary General Kofi Annan.

Ultimately, the NATO heads of state decided to endorse a "peace-enforcing" role for NATO in Afghanistan and for NATO to assume control of the ISAF mission. France, which had opposed such a move earlier, already had forces on the ground in Afghanistan as part of the ISAF mission and now agreed to NATO's role under the condition that its forces would continue their peacekeeping role in the Kabul

---

[4] For more background on this resistance, see Chapter Three, pp. 16–18.

[5] Judy Dempsey, "France Bars Moves for Greater Alliance Role," *Financial Times*, February 10, 2003.

[6] See, for example, George Robertson, "Speech by NATO Secretary General Lord Robertson to the NATO Parliamentary Assembly," NATO Online Library, May 26, 2003.

[7] General Götz Gliemeroth, ISAF Commander, "Interview," *NATO Review*, Winter 2003.

area. Furthermore, France, while adamantly against a NATO role in Iraq, agreed that adding NATO's full support in a stabilization and peacekeeping role in Afghanistan would add more security than the existing ISAF mission could provide the country. The move was viewed as an opportunity to show NATO's commitment, as a cohesive group, to adapting to the demands of the 21st century. As Supreme Allied Commander, Europe, General Jones noted, this NATO decision made "a clear statement of transition, from the 20th century defensive bipolar world, into the multipolar flexible need for rapid response across a myriad of threats."[8] Following this decision, NATO assumed control of ISAF indefinitely on August 11, 2003. NATO, for the first time ever in its over 50-year history, was conducting an operation outside Europe.

NATO in Command of the International Security Assistance Force

In August 2003, NATO's command of ISAF officially began in Kabul, Afghanistan. NATO's commitment was envisaged as unfolding in five phases:

1. assessment and preparation
2. geographic expansion
3. stabilization
4. transition
5. redeployment.[9]

After completing Phase 1 within a few months of arriving in Afghanistan, NATO forces entered Phase 2 and considered enlarging their presence throughout the country. On October 13, 2003, UN Security Council Resolution (UNSCR) 1510 passed, officially expand-

[8] "Putting Things in Order: In a Dangerous and Unstable World, NATO Finds New Purpose," *Ottawa Citizen*, August 12, 2003.

[9] NATO, "International Security Assistance Force (ISAF): Key Facts and Figures," fact sheet with map, July 6, 2010e.

ing NATO's role outside the vicinity of Kabul.[10] Two days later, the NRF, described as "a quick-reaction force for hostage-rescue, peace interventions, and combat operations far from Europe," was declared ready for use.[11] Initially, some in NATO touted the NRF as a capability that could even be used in Afghanistan; Secretary General Jaap de Hoop Scheffer, for example, declared the NRF to be "easy to send to any theater the allies would like it sent to."[12] Others, however, expressed reservations. Despite the internal debate about where, when, and why the NRF would be deployed, its declared readiness fueled the argument that NATO possessed the needed capabilities and capacity to take on an expanded role in Afghanistan, thereby lending credence to the idea of further expanding NATO's presence.[13] As a result, NATO forces continued to prepare for a growing security role in northern Afghanistan even as the internal debate ensued. This, however, was only the first of several stages of NATO expansion throughout the country. Table 1 outlines this and subsequent mission expansions into other areas of responsibility.

Table 1
NATO Areas of Responsibility in Afghanistan

Stage	Regions	Date Completed
1	Kabul and North	October 2004
2	Kabul, North, and West	September 2005
3	Kabul, North, West, and South	July 31, 2006
4	Kabul, North, West, South, and East	October 5, 2006

SOURCE: NATO, 2010d.

---

[10] See UNSCR 1510, on the expanding mission of the International Security Force, October 13, 2003.

[11] Nicholas Burns, "Transforming NATO's Role," *Boston Globe*, December 22, 2003.

[12] "Afghanistan: NATO Chief Not Ruling Out More Alliance Involvement," Radio Free Europe/Radio Liberty, October 13, 2004.

[13] Note, however, that the NRF was only used for a limited role in Afghanistan to provide security during the Afghan elections in 2004.

By summer 2006, NATO's role had expanded from Kabul (the capital) and the northern areas of Afghanistan to include its western and southern areas as well. The only area that was beyond NATO's reach was the highly unstable east, which remained under U.S. control and included the largely ungoverned border areas of Afghanistan and Pakistan, where remaining Taliban forces were known to reside and stage attacks on NATO and Afghan forces.[14] Even as NATO's area of responsibility expanded to the south, plans were already under way for the alliance to assume responsibility for the entire country.

However, completing this last step would require careful coordination between NATO and U.S. forces operating primarily in the east under OEF. Coordination was also required inside the U.S. command structure, between the NATO commander—who also commands U.S. European Command—and the commander of U.S. Central Command, who was responsible for U.S. forces engaged in OEF. Although command responsibilities remain blurred to this day, sufficient progress was made by fall 2006 for NATO to assume responsibility for all of Afghanistan, but with sensitive counterterrorist responsibilities remaining under U.S. control.

In the span of two short years, NATO's role in Afghanistan expanded from a tentative commitment to stabilization and reconstruction in limited parts of the country to responsibility for the security of the entire country. Yet, despite some voiced concerns,[15] it is unclear whether NATO itself completely understood the full extent of this commitment and the risks it would entail. Even official declarations of the enhanced NATO-ISAF partnership with Afghanistan

---

[14] See Seth G. Jones, "The State of the Afghan Insurgency," testimony presented before the Canadian Senate National Security and Defence Committee on December 10, 2007, Santa Monica, Calif.: RAND Corporation, CT-296, 2007, p. 6.

[15] Germany, Britain, and France all voiced concerns about merging the NATO peacekeeping and U.S. combat missions in Afghanistan. See Seth G. Jones, *In the Graveyard of Empires: America's War in Afghanistan*, New York: W.W. Norton & Company, 2009, p. 249, and Judy Dempsey and David S. Cloud, "Europeans Balking at New Afghan Role," *New York Times*, September 14, 2005.

avoided discussing combat.[16] Indeed, the focus was on Afghan efforts to become competent at all levels of governance rather than on Afghan primary dependence on ISAF for security:

> Afghanistan recognises that at present it is unable to fully meet its own security needs and highly appreciates NATO's contribution to providing security and stability in Afghanistan. Afghanistan is determined to develop rapidly the capabilities of its national security and defence institutions to meet national requirements, operate more effectively alongside ISAF and international military forces, and improve their capacity for independent action.[17]

Indeed, two years was all it took for NATO in Afghanistan to take over the security mission, yet in some sense, NATO in Brussels seemed years behind.

As NATO's responsibilities grew, so too did its structure and organization. The NATO-ISAF organization includes several main elements: a headquarters in Kabul, an air task force, and five regional commands that coordinate and provide command and control for the 26 Provincial Reconstruction Teams (PRTs). The PRTs, most led by one ISAF country with support from others, have several subcomponents (security, reconstruction, a steering committee, and support framework) and play an instrumental role in security and reconstruction efforts.[18]

Together, Figure 1 and Table 2 illustrate the distribution of PRTs and regional commands across Afghanistan and identify the nations leading them.

The roles and responsibilities of various NATO members on the ground in Afghanistan have evolved over time.[19] For example, the

---

[16] North Atlantic Treaty Organisation and the Islamic Republic of Afghanistan, "Declaration," NATO Basic Text, September 6, 2006

[17] North Atlantic Treaty Organisation and the Islamic Republic of Afghanistan, 2006.

[18] For more information on PRTs, including the official mission statement, see NATO, "ISAF Provincial Reconstruction Teams (PRTs)," undated.

[19] Note that roles and responsibilities are affected by such factors as national caveats, as well as NATO and U.S. operational factors. See Chapter Five for a discussion of these factors and limitations.

Figure 1
ISAF Regional Commands and Provincial Reconstruction Team Locations

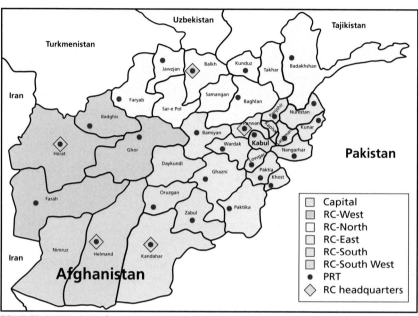

SOURCE: NATO, 2010d.
RAND *MG974-1*

Table 2
Distribution and Lead Nations

Regional Command		Location	Lead Nation
West	Command headquarters	Herat	Italy
	Forward support base	Herat	Spain
	PRTs	Herat	Italy
		Farah	United States
		Qala-e-Now	Spain
		Chaghcharan	Lithuania
North	Command headquarters	Mazar-e-Sharif	Germany
	Forward support base	Mazar-e-Sharif	Germany
	PRTs	Mazar-e-Sharif	Sweden
		Feyzabad	Germany
		Kunduz	Germany
		Pol-e-Khomri	Hungary

Table 2—Continued

Regional Command		Location	Lead Nation
		Meymaneh	Norway
		Jowzjan	Turkey
Capital	Command headquarters	Kabul	Turkey
	Kabul International Airport	Kabul	Spain
East	Command headquarters	Bagram	United States
	Forward support base	Bagram	United States
	PRTs	Logar	Czechoslovakia
		Sharana	United States
		Khost	United States
		Mether Lam	United States
		Bamyan	New Zealand
		Panjshir	United States
		Jalalabad	United States
		Ghazni	United States
		Asadabad	United States
		Bagram	United States
		Nuristan	United States
		Wardak	Turkey
		Gardez	United States
		Parwan	Korea
South	Command headquarters	Kandahar	United Kingdom
	Forward support base	Kandahar	United Kingdom
	PRTs	Kandahar	Canada
		Tarin Kowt	Netherlands
		Qalat	United States
South West	Command headquarters	Lashkar Gah	United Kingdom
	Forward support base	Kandahar	United Kingdom
	PRTs	Lashkar Gah	United Kingdom

SOURCE: NATO, 2010d.

United States has deployed a significant number of ground forces, primarily to eastern Afghanistan (under both the ISAF and OEF umbrellas), as well as U.S. air support and various intelligence, surveillance, and reconnaissance assets. Similarly, the UK has contributed ground forces (largely stationed in the south, with approximately 500 special forces contributing to OEF) supported by a number of UK aircraft, such as heavy-lift helicopters and attack helicopters.[20] Also contributing to Regional Command South is Canada with its armored, infantry, and reconnaissance forces, and support from unmanned aerial vehicles. In addition, Dutch ground forces stationed a sizeable presence primarily in the central province of Uruzgan (approximately 1,955 as of July 2010), with support from attack helicopters and transport support.[21] Each of the above-mentioned countries engages in a number of counterinsurgency operations in the volatile southern and eastern regions. Germany's forces, which include special forces, are stationed in the north and play an important role in training the Afghan National Security Forces (ANSF) and in reconstruction efforts. Also assisting with these efforts in the north are French and Italian forces. French ground forces are aided by fighters, tankers, and transport aircraft. Italian forces (also located in the west) are supported by several utility and attack helicopters and by unmanned aerial vehicles.

Since the onset of ISAF operations, reconstruction and development efforts have made measurable, yet tenuous, progress in several areas. For example, numerous infrastructure projects have resulted in the construction or repair of approximately 20,000 km of roads and over 3,500 schools (with over 7 million children now in school).[22] In addition, development programs, many of which are Afghan-led, have decreased infant and under-five mortality rates, and more Afghans have access to health care.[23] Overall, ongoing countrywide efforts and funding are focused on a broad spectrum of efforts, such as rebuilding and improving hospitals, schools, and bridges; increasing access to water and electricity; and decreasing poppy cultivation.

---

[20] Kenneth Katzman, "Afghanistan: Post-Taliban Governance, Security, and U.S. Policy," Washington, D.C.: Congressional Research Service, December 30, 2009, p. 43.

[21] NATO, 2010d. Dutch forces ended their deployment in Afghanistan in August 2010, handing their command over to the United States and Australia. See "Dutch Troops End Afghanistan Deployment," BBC News, August 1, 2010.

[22] NATO, "Afghanistan Report 2009," 2009a, pp. 32 and 37.

[23] NATO, 2008c.

ISAF forces also play a vital role in supporting the growth of the ANSF through the NATO Training Mission–Afghanistan (NTM-A). This role includes training the Afghan National Army (ANA) and the Afghan National Police (ANP).[24] ISAF support to the ANSF includes training, equipping, and mentoring, as well as substantial financial resources. The United States leads the ANA training program through the Combined Security Transition Command–Afghanistan with support from ISAF nations.[25] The ANP training program has been reformed several times. In 2002, Germany's Police Project Office was in the lead; in 2007, the EU Police Mission (EUPOL) in Afghanistan had it. Then, in 2009, NTM-A was established to oversee the effort, allowing police operational mentoring and liaison teams (POMLTs) to focus on training at the district level and below and EUPOL to focus on higher-level efforts (management, standards, etc.).[26]

The objective of both the ANA and ANP efforts is to develop the size and strength of the ANSF so that they can effectively function on their own to provide security for the entire country. However, from the onset of the mission, reaching ANSF's manpower objectives has been hampered by a lack of resources and capabilities and an inadequate number of trainers. In May 2007, reports criticized the progress and lack of growth of the ANSF, noting in particular that neither the ANA nor ANP were "fully capable of operating independently" and that only a fraction of the units were capable of leading operations with support from coalition forces.[27] Subsequent steps to address such shortcomings and reform ANSF development efforts have produced

---

[24] NATO, "Backgrounder: NATO Training Mission—Afghanistan (NTM-A)," Brussels: NATO Public Diplomacy Division, April 2010a.

[25] For more on efforts to build the ANA, see Obaid Younossi, Peter Dahl Thruelsen, Jonathan Vaccaro, Jerry M. Sollinger, and Brian Grady, *The Long March: Building an Afghan National Army*, Santa Monica, Calif.: RAND Corporation, MG-845-RDCC/OSD, 2009; NATO, "Fact Sheet: ANA Equipment Support," February 2008b.

[26] As of June 2010, NATO had fielded 37 POMLTs, and the United States had fielded 279 POMLTs. See NATO, "Facts & Figures: Afghan National Army," Brussels: NATO Public Diplomacy Division, June 2010b, and NATO, 2010a.

[27] U.S. Government Accountability Office, "Securing, Stabilizing, and Reconstructing Afghanistan: Key Issues for Congressional Oversight," Washington, D.C., May 2007, p. 14.

some progress. As of May 2010, the ANA numbered 119,388 troops (with a goal of 171,600 by October 2011), was actively participating in the majority of ISAF operations, and was leading over 60 percent of joint operations.[28] Nevertheless, Afghan forces remain heavily reliant on support from U.S. and coalition forces. In comparison, also as of May 2010, there were 104,459 ANP (with a goal of 134,000 by October 2011).[29] Yet, despite the continued growth in overall security forces, the pace of training continues to lag, and ANSF has more progress to make toward becoming sufficiently trained, resourced, and equipped to provide security for such a vast area without relying on significant assistance from the United States or ISAF.

In light of these challenges, many NATO members called for an improved and reenergized training mission in Afghanistan. In early 2008, U.S. Secretary of Defense Robert Gates noted:

> I think that the principal shortfall—continuing shortfall—will be in having as many trainers as we would like for the security forces, but we have responded.[30]

Even two years later, pleas continued for more resources to support the training mission.[31]

As previously noted, the EU assumed the lead role for training the Afghan police in May 2007 prior to the establishment of NTM-A; however, this mission was fraught with complications because of a number of disputes inside the EU. For example, Turkey has made NATO–EU cooperation difficult on several occasions, such as by blocking efforts

---

[28] NATO, "Facts & Figures: Afghan National Army," Brussels: NATO Public Diplomacy Division, December 2009d; NATO, 2010b.

[29] See NATO, "Facts & Figures: Afghan National Police," December 2009, and "Communiqué," Afghanistan: The London Conference, January 28, 2010.

[30] Tom Bowman, "U.S. Military Falls Short of Afghan Training Goals," *All Things Considered*, National Public Radio, January 25, 2008; Soraya Sarhaddi Nelson, "U.S. Launches Aggressive Training for Afghan Police," *All Things Considered*, National Public Radio, March 17, 2008.

[31] Luke Baker and Andrew Quinn, "NATO Allies Offer 7,000 Extra Troops for Afghan War," Reuters, December 4, 2009.

to share NATO intelligence with the EU and Afghan police forces because some countries (e.g., Cyprus) were not NATO members.[32] Such disputes, coupled with NATO's inability to provide adequate numbers of trainers, have limited the alliance's ability to meet its goals for the ANA and ANP, and ultimately undermine NATO's broader goal of creating a viable Afghan security force at local, regional, and national levels.[33] NATO has consistently missed its goals, leaving little confidence that it will meet its future targets.[34] Given that the creation of a viable and self-sustaining Afghan security force is perhaps the one key development that would allow NATO to reduce its commitments over time, it remains perplexing and disconcerting that NATO has consistently fallen short on such a crucial undertaking.

In the absence of mature Afghan security forces, NATO has been maintaining a steady presence in country to counter resurgent Taliban forces. Many, if not all, of the Taliban forces have been staging from inside ungoverned Pakistani territory. NATO and U.S. forces have been involved in a series of controversial operations along the Afghan-Pakistan border areas, including air attacks against suspected Taliban forces inside Pakistan. As spring 2007 arrived, NATO commanders prepared for what they believed would be a major Taliban offensive, but it failed to materialize, and NATO forces faced only sporadic fighting in the south and along the eastern border.[35] Nevertheless, one year

---

[32] See, for example, Paul Gallis, "NATO in Afghanistan: A Test of the Transatlantic Alliance," Washington, D.C.: Congressional Research Service, October 23, 2007, p. 14.

[33] NATO's inability to meet its goals for training the ANA and ANP has led to finger-pointing in the alliance. Germany, for one, has borne the brunt of criticism for its inadequate training of Afghan police in particular. See Seth G. Jones, "Getting Back on Track in Afghanistan," testimony presented before the House Foreign Affairs Committee, Subcommittee on the Middle East and South Asia, on April 2, 2008, Santa Monica, Calif.: RAND Corporation, CT-301, April 2008, p. 3; Judy Dempsey, "Germany Assailed for Training Afghan Police Poorly," *New York Times*, November 15, 2006.

[34] At NATO's London Conference in January 2010, the stated goal was to have Afghans control the physical security of Afghanistan within five years. See "Communiqué," 2010, and Alistair MacDonald, Matthew Rosenberg, and Jay Solomon, "Nations Outline Afghan Security Shift," *Wall Street Journal*, January 29, 2010.

[35] See, for example, Susanne Koelbl, "NATO Battles Rising Hostility in Afghanistan," *Der Spiegel*, March 13, 2007.

later, echoes of a looming spring offensive resumed and, this time, the warnings rang more true. Taliban attacks increased, and the border area grew ever more contested. Taliban attacks intensified greatly in 2009 and 2010. While NATO forces have shown their commitment to providing and improving security, the continued violence and attacks have led senior civilian and military leaders to revisit NATO's strategy for Afghanistan several times.[36]

The Broader Challenge

The resurgent Taliban remain a serious and real hindrance to progress, but only one part of the broader challenge: Reconstruction efforts continue to lag; training of the Afghan army and police is, at best, a work in progress; and corruption continues to plague government services throughout the country. The status of certain specific areas of concern can be summarized briefly:

- **Governance.** Effective governance in Afghanistan remains a key component of U.S. strategy there, yet reaching this goal continues to be a struggle.[37] In 2009, U.S. officials estimated that President Karzai's government has control of only 30 percent of Afghanistan, with insurgents controlling approximately 4 percent and having influence in an additional 30 percent; the remaining areas are under the control of tribes or local groups.[38] The controversial presidential and provincial elections in 2009 (ending with the inauguration of President Karzai on November 19, 2009) and continued widespread corruption are indicative of the challenges UN and NATO officials have faced in establishing an effective

---

[36] A number of reviews have been done, such as those by General Petraeus (October 2008), General McChrystal (August 2009), and the U.S. administration (March 2009 and December 2009).

[37] Kenneth Katzman, "Afghanistan: Politics, Elections, and Government Performance," Washington, D.C.: Congressional Research Service, September 14, 2010.

[38] Katzman, 2009, p. 23.

governance structure across all levels given the balance of power between local tribes and the national government.

- **Narcotics.** Narcotics in Afghanistan continue to account for the majority of Taliban funds (an estimated $70 million to 100 million annually).[39] While counternarcotic efforts have helped reduce opium cultivation by 22 percent in 2009, Afghanistan still accounted for an estimated 93 percent of the world's opium supply.[40] More provinces were declared "poppy free" in 2009 (20 provinces, compared to 18 in 2008 and 13 in 2007). Yet some of the most volatile areas still produce large amounts of the crop (e.g., Helmand), and other provinces previously declared "poppy free" are now back to producing poppy.[41] Counternarcotic efforts range from agricultural initiatives that aim to identify alternatives to poppy production to efforts that combat the narcotics trade more directly by targeting the funding chain and drug traffickers.[42]

- **Violence.** 2010 was the most violent year in Afghanistan to date, with more than 600 coalition fatalities (of which more than 400 were U.S. service members, and more than 90 were UK service members).[43] Security incidents continue to occur at a high rate, being 69 percent higher in a given month in 2010 than in the same month in 2009.[44] Attacks averaged 1,100 per month in 2009, compared to 1,000 per month in 2008, 800 per month in 2007, 800 per month in 2006, and 400 in 2005.[45] Impro-

---

[39] Katzman, 2009, p. 20.

[40] Katzman, 2009, p. 20. These reductions in opium cultivation, however, may not continue. See Kenneth Katzman, "Afghanistan: Post-Taliban Governance, Security, and U.S. Policy," Washington, D.C.: Congressional Research Service, July 21, 2010, p. 21.

[41] Katzman, 2009, p. 20.

[42] In October 2008, NATO received additional authority to target drug runners and drug labs. See Fawzia Sheikh, "DoD Official: Confidence in Afghan Counterdrug Police Will Grow," *Inside the Pentagon*, October 16, 2008; and Katzman, 2010, p. 22.

[43] See icasualties.org, OEF web page, various dates.

[44] UN, 2010.

[45] Katzman, 2010, p. 55.

vised explosive devices continue to pose a high threat, with an 82-percent increase in 2010 compared to the same period in 2009.[46] Furthermore, improvised explosive devices accounted for 7,000 attacks in 2009 and 4,900 attacks over just the first five months of 2010.[47] Suicide bombings also remain one of the Taliban's weapons of choice (over 200 bombings in 2008 compared to 160 in 2007, 123 in 2006, and 21 in 2005).[48] However, the majority of the violence (70 percent) in Afghanistan occurs in a small percentage of the country (10 percent), with an additional percentage originating in the ungoverned areas of Pakistan.[49]

While this list is not exhaustive, it highlights the scope of the challenges NATO forces continue to face. Additionally, as NATO moves forward, it will need to address each of these challenges comprehensively as part of a long-term strategy for success in Afghanistan that is coordinated with other key powers, including the Afghan government, the UN, and the EU.

---

[46] UN, 2010.

[47] Anthony H. Cordesman and Jason Lemieux, "IED Metrics for Afghanistan: January 2004–May 2010," Washington, D.C.: CSIS, July 21, 2010.

[48] Katzman, 2009, p. 50.

[49] See NATO, 2009a; Katzman, 2010, p. 27.

CHAPTER FIVE

Risking NATO in Afghanistan

At the close of a conference of Army leaders from 38 European nations in Germany in October 2007, U.S. Secretary of Defense Gates spoke out in frustration:

> If an alliance of the world's greatest democracies cannot summon the will to get the job done in a mission that we agree is morally just and vital to our security, then our citizens may begin to question both the worth of the mission and the utility of the 60-year-old trans-Atlantic security project itself.[1]

Gates, of course, was focusing on how to generate additional commitments from NATO's European members, but in a different sense, Gates pointed to a genuine paradox surrounding NATO's role in Afghanistan: NATO might ultimately succeed in Afghanistan but fail as an alliance. Despite the ups and downs of NATO's performance in Afghanistan and despite the actual circumstances in Afghanistan on any given day, it is clear that NATO has committed itself to a mission that is unlike anything the alliance has experienced in the past and that will test the alliance for all it is worth.

It was not at all inevitable that NATO would decide to become involved in Afghanistan—who among NATO's founders would have envisioned such a step?—but it was also not particularly surprising.

---

[1] "Afghanistan: Gates Doubts Europeans' War Commitment," *New York Times*, October 26, 2007. As requests for more resources remained unanswered, U.S. calls for more allied support slowly diminished. See John Vinocur, "U.S. Gives Absolution to Its Allies," *New York Times*, June 2, 2009.

Given the turmoil in the alliance during the past decade, particularly over the war in Iraq, Afghanistan provided an opportunity for the alliance to act in unison to meet a pressing need; to show its relevance in dealing with a new type of security challenge; and to deflect growing criticism, coming mostly (although not exclusively) from the United States, that NATO lacked the capacity to act and was becoming little more than a high-priced debating society. In short, Afghanistan provided an opportunity to demonstrate that NATO was still capable of "doing something."

Yet, by doing something, NATO also learned that its problems amounted to more than just the security situation in Afghanistan. By committing itself to a long-term, out-of-area operation, NATO soon learned, and indeed continues to learn, that it also needs to devote considerably more attention to managing risks at home—that is, in the council of the transatlantic alliance. NATO's renewed debate about risks has moved well beyond mounting a successful defense of Western Europe and has become centered on sharing risks and burdens more equitably, including troop commitments to NATO missions inside and outside NATO territory.[2]

For the first time in NATO history, the discussion of risks and burdens includes the immediate risk of casualties. It also includes the relative roles of various NATO and non-NATO members in emerging alliance missions and more-effective ways of managing the expectations of NATO's military commanders, political leaders, and publics.

Sharing Burdens

Since their first days in Afghanistan, NATO's military commanders have felt starved for resources—troops and equipment—although this feeling is not at all new in the history of NATO debates. NATO has long struggled to generate resources commensurate with the missions it has taken on, and episodes of finger-pointing at those who were thought not

---

[2]   Many, however, still worry about Russian harassment and intimidation, such as the apparently Russian-sponsored cyber attacks against Estonia in May of 2007.

to be sharing equitably in the burdens have been frequent.[3] As Figure 2 illustrates, the burdens in Afghanistan, particularly in terms of troop contributions, have not been shared equitably, to say the least; most of the burden has fallen on a few key members and, importantly, several non-NATO members. As the figure shows, the United States currently contributes the greatest number of troops to the ISAF mission. As of May 2010, the estimated number of U.S. forces in theater was 94,000 (and estimated to increase to 98,000 by the end of 2010), approximately 78,400 supporting ISAF.[4] In comparison, NATO forces (excluding U.S. forces) supporting ISAF as of July 2010 totaled about 37,500.[5] The 35 European countries supporting ISAF currently account for about 35,600 of these troops.[6] Without question, total U.S. forces clearly comprise the majority of coalition forces in theater—double the amount of European forces—and U.S. force contributions to ISAF alone are equivalent to over 50 percent of total ISAF forces.

Going back to late 2007 and early 2008, the debate over troop commitments had intensified greatly. Military commanders found themselves in the all-too-familiar and frustrating position of asking for more troops and equipment. NATO's Supreme Allied Commander at the time, General Craddock, echoed the views of his predecessor:

> We are not losing, we are just not winning fast enough. I am convinced that if we had what we need that we would see more

---

[3] In 1988, the U.S. Congress voted to amend a bill "to require the phased withdrawal of U.S. troops stationed in Europe. . . . unless those countries collectively increase their defense spending as a percentage of gross national product to a level equivalent to that of the United States." Although it did not pass, it highlights a long-standing debate on addressing inequities of defense spending between the United States and Europe. (Library of Congress, Bill Summary & Status, 100th Congress [1987–1988]: H.AMDT.628, 1988.)

[4] The United States also has troops deployed as part of OEF. Anne Gearan, "More U.S. Troops in Afghanistan than Iraq," Associated Press, May 24, 2010; NATO, 2010d. U.S. President Barack Obama authorized an additional 30,000 troops to support the mission in December 2009. See Barack Obama, "Address to the Nation on the Way Forward in Afghanistan and Pakistan," Washington, D.C.: The White House, Office of the Press Secretary, December 1, 2009.

[5] NATO, 2010d.

[6] NATO, 2010d.

Figure 2
Current Troop Contributions to ISAF

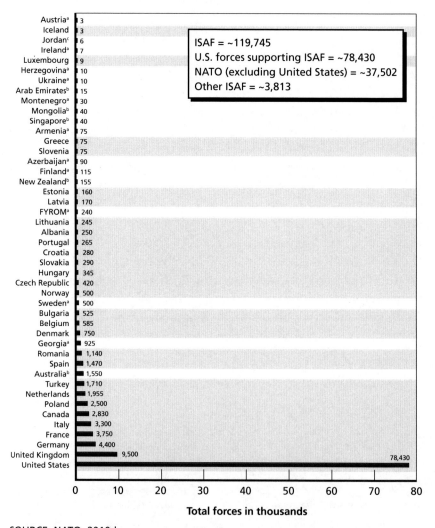

SOURCE: NATO, 2010d.
NOTE: Shading denotes NATO members.
[a] NATO partner nations
[b] Non-NATO, non–Euro-Atlantic Partnership Council nations
[c] Mediterranean dialogue country
RAND *MG974-2*

progress. Look, the fact of the matter is the opposing militant forces operate in the space between what we have and what we need. Fill the space up and you take away their operating space. Advantage, NATO.[7]

This time, however, the pleading was accompanied by calls from American political leaders. Secretary of Defense Robert Gates pleaded and cajoled in public and private, but with little success. A response from then–German Defense Minister Franz Josef Jung was typical: ". . . our contribution is excellent,"[8] implying that more need not and would not be done.

Seemingly out of frustration, the United States was signaling that it would make up part of the troop shortfall on its own by committing an additional 3,000 Marines to Afghanistan. But this only added to tensions in NATO over European partners' unwillingness or inability to generate sufficient forces to contend with a highly volatile security situation, not just in Afghanistan but also now in neighboring Pakistan. This, in turn, led even more American skeptics to wonder whether investments in cultivating partners in NATO were worth the effort, given what some thought to be so little in return.[9]

Indeed, some in the United States came to question why NATO should maintain a voice on key decisions in Afghanistan— particularly key warfighting decisions—when the United States seemed to be getting so little in return for sharing responsibility with its NATO partners. These dissenters suggested revisiting the division of labor in Afghanistan so that the United States could reclaim control over operations in Afghanistan's south and east, which in turn would give the United States the primary voice on operations against Taliban

---

[7] Al Pessin, "NATO Commander Says More Troops Needed in Afghanistan," Voice of America, February 10, 2008.

[8] "NATO States Wrangle Over Troop Commitments," Agence France Presse, February 7, 2008.

[9] See, for example, Andrew J. Bacevich, "NATO at Twilight," Los Angeles Times, February 11, 2008. Bacevich's conclusion is: "It's time to jettison the capital letters: NATO has become nato."

insurgents and al Qaeda forces operating out of Pakistan and along the border.[10]

By late 2008, the tone of the debate had changed. A consensus was growing inside NATO that Afghanistan was starved for troops and that more personnel would need to be committed. But estimates of what was required overwhelmed what NATO members had to offer. Renewed calls for additional troops from the U.S. secretaries of State and Defense yielded fairly little in return.[11] As American politics focused on the 2008 presidential campaign, both major candidates were promising additional troops for Afghanistan, but even these promises seemed to fall considerably short of what commanders on the ground thought would be needed to contend with the vastly expanded Taliban threat.

The writing was on the wall, and the United States could not wait. Too much was at stake, and the resurgent Taliban threat was putting their efforts—and lives—at risk. With U.S. operations in Iraq beginning to wind down, the United States found itself in a position where it could shift its focus back to Afghanistan, along with significantly more resources. Calls for a renewed U.S. effort in Afghanistan grew louder—"Success in Afghanistan will require a reassertion of U.S. leadership"[12]—and action soon followed. The Americanization of the war in Afghanistan began in early 2009 with an announcement by President Obama that the United States would be sending an additional 17,000 troops and culminated in December 2009 when President Obama authorized the deployment of an additional 30,000 troops by the summer of 2010.

This strategy shift was punctuated early on with the swift dismissal of General David McKiernan as the top commander in Afghanistan in May 2009 by U.S. Secretary of Defense Gates. Gen McKiernan

---

[10] Robert Burns, "Pentagon May Beef Up Afghanistan Command Role," Associated Press, May 1, 2008.

[11] See, for example, Dan Bilefsky, "Europe Asked to Send Afghanistan More Troops," *New York Times*, October 8, 2008.

[12] Lt Gen David W. Barno, testimony before the Senate Armed Services Committee, Washington, D.C., February 26, 2009.

would be replaced by then–Lieutenant General Stanley McChrystal, who would soon be promoted to general. This overhaul marked a significant change—one driven by "a need for new leadership" and for "fresh thinking, fresh eyes on the problem."[13] Indeed, fresh thinking was one resource they had in abundance. The initial wave of American resources and influence into Afghanistan in spring and summer 2009 was followed by ideas on how operations should be organized and the strategy reformulated. Although the United States was looking to fill a void left by unmet calls for more resources, U.S. leaders were quick to reiterate the continued importance of coalition contributions in the overall mission. But the role the coalition would play was brought back to the discussion table, with some reviving arguments for a division of labor. The proposals varied, ranging from a bifurcation of ISAF into a peacekeeping contingent and warfighting contingent, to a shift in ISAF responsibility back to the north and west to allow a coalition of the willing to control the east and south (i.e., "turning back the clock").[14]

The debate continued through summer 2009 after General McChrystal released his own assessment of the situation in Afghanistan accompanied by a request for more resources to complete the mission.[15] This ultimately led to the second wave of American resources, initiated by President Obama's decision on December 1, 2009, to authorize the deployment of an additional 30,000 troops to support the mission. Without question, the Americanization of the effort would help revive the Afghan mission and take some pressure off NATO allies,

---

[13] Secretary of Defense Robert M. Gates and Chairman of the Joint Chiefs of Staff Adm. Michael Mullen, "Leadership Changes in Afghanistan from the Pentagon," press conference transcript, Washington, D.C.: U.S. Department of Defense, Office of the Assistant Secretary of Defense (Public Affairs), May 11, 2009.

[14] See Thomas Donnelly, "Coalition Still Critical as America Escalates Afghan War," *Washington Examiner*, June 16, 2009, and Joseph J. Collins, "Afghanistan: The Path to Victory," *Joint Forces Quarterly*, No. 54, 3rd Qtr. 2009.

[15] General Stanley A. McChrystal, "COMISAF's Initial Assessment," Kabul, Afghanistan: Headquarters, International Security Assistance Force, August 30, 2009. See also Eric Schmitt and Thom Shanker, "General Calls for More U.S. Troops to Avoid Afghan Failure," *New York Times*, September 20, 2009.

but what remains unanswered is whether it would be enough. Indeed, subsequent leadership changes further added to this uncertainty. In a relatively quick turn of events, General McChrystal was relieved of command in June 2010 and replaced by General David Petraeus, who initiated a new review of the operational strategy. This change also prompted a renewed debate about alternative strategies.

Moreover, the underlying issue of troops and equipment has renewed a long-standing NATO discussion about money, specifically over who in NATO is spending what for defense. As Figure 3 indicates, 2009 defense spending estimates show that only four NATO members met NATO's unofficial spending floor of at least 2 percent of gross domestic product on defense, with several members spending less for defense now than they did even a few years ago (as the bars denoting annual spending indicate). Consequently, the burden-sharing debate has become more pointed since NATO took responsibility for ISAF and Afghanistan more generally and continues despite the recent Americanization of the effort. As operational demands in Afghanistan increase, some would expect such demands to increase defense spending; however, the absence of, and, in some cases, the reverse of such a trend may be viewed as an indicator of a lack of support for the mission in Afghanistan and may endanger the cohesion of the alliance more broadly.

But in a broader sense, debates over troops, equipment, and money mask the real burden-sharing debate now taking place in NATO: casualties. NATO debates in decades past about "fighting to the last European" were always theoretical. Even in the 1990s, when NATO contemplated involvement in Bosnia and Kosovo, the matter of casualties loomed in the shadows but never really came into the open.[16] But Afghanistan is something altogether different. For the first time in its history, NATO forces are suffering casualties, and for the first time

---

[16] Perhaps telling of the possible effects of NATO casualties on operations in Afghanistan, a Dutch F-16 (flying air defense combat air patrols over the U.S. attacking force) shot down a Serbian MiG early in the Kosovo conflict. This prompted European television reporters to wonder if the shoot-down would cause the Serbian government to collapse. However, when the Dutch lost an attack helicopter in Afghanistan, they stood down their in-country aviation for a few days. (Conversation with Colonel (ret.) Joseph Collins, July 2009.)

Figure 3
NATO Member Defense Expenditures as a Percentage of Gross Domestic Product (2005–2009)

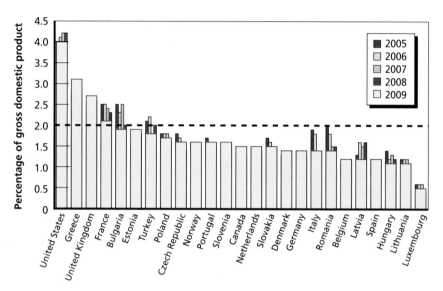

SOURCE: Supplied by NATO Public Policy Division, 2010.
RAND *MG974-3*

in its history, NATO's political leaders have been forced to consider not just who provides troops, equipment, and money but who will be willing to give lives in the defense of common interests. In a very real sense, NATO has been forced to confront not only who shares what burdens but who shares what risks. What was once a theoretical debate has become all too real and has resulted in profound cleavages in the alliance.

These cleavages came clearly to the fore as American, British, Canadian, and Dutch leaders, while answering to their own publics, began calling for other NATO partners to share more in NATO's risks in Afghanistan.[17] Much of the initial frustration was heaped on Germany, with calls for German forces to take on greater roles in Afghanistan, including fighting roles, and sparking an intense political debate

---

[17] This pressure began in 2006 but intensified through 2007 and continued through the April 2008 NATO Summit in Bucharest, Romania.

in Germany itself. The weekly *Der Spiegel* went so far as to suggest, "Germans have to learn how to kill." The report went on to note, "NATO, which sees itself as the world's most powerful military alliance, faces the real possibility of political and possibly even military defeat in its bloody war of attrition with the Taliban."[18] Pressures on Germany, both internally and externally, continue to this day.[19]

With little success thus far in attracting more NATO commitments, particularly commitments to Afghanistan's most dangerous areas,[20] such allies as Canada have found themselves faced with the grim reality that they were suffering a greater number of casualties relative to their total force size in comparison to other NATO members. Figure 4 shows that, while the United States has lost the greatest number of soldiers in Afghanistan overall (over 1,216 fatalities since October 2001[21]), these losses account for a smaller fraction of its overall national force than losses other countries, such as Canada, the UK, Estonia, and Denmark, have suffered. NATO leaders have thus far been able to deflect some of the harshest terms of the casualty sharing debate, but it is not inconceivable that, even in the near future, some NATO members could claim to be absorbing a much higher percentage of risk because their forces are taking more casualties in Afghanistan on a proportionate basis of total national forces. NATO leaders have yet to find the right terms for this debate, but they will need to do so if they are to maintain support for the mission and if they are to account for who is sharing what burdens and assuming what risks in meeting overall alliance commitments.

---

[18] Konstantin von Hammerstein, "The Germans Have to Learn How to Kill," *Der Spiegel*, November 20, 2006.

[19] For example, in December 2008, General Hans-Christoph Ammon, who headed the German Army's special commando unit, labeled German efforts to train the Afghan police as "a miserable failure." See Judy Dempsey, "German General Criticizes Nation's Efforts in Afghanistan," *Boston Globe*, December 1, 2008.

[20] Indeed, the Americanization of the effort in 2009 is a seeming admission of this reality. See also Craig Whitlock, "NATO Hits Snags on Troop Pledges," *Washington Post*, January 27, 2010.

[21] icasualties website, August 6, 2010.

Figure 4
Coalition Fatalities per 100,000 in Total National Armed Force

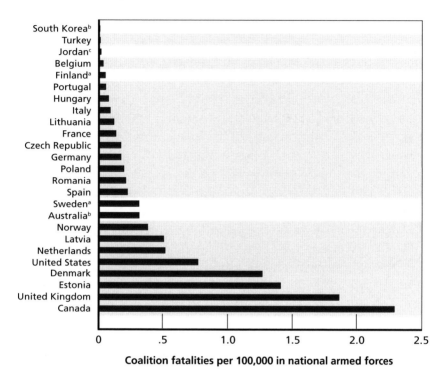

Coalition fatalities per 100,000 in national armed forces

SOURCES: International Institute for Strategic Studies, *The Military Balance*,
Vol. 110, No. 1, February 2010, pp. 462–468; icasualties.org, 2010.
NOTE: Shading denotes NATO members.
[a] NATO partner nations
[b] Non-NATO, non–Euro-Atlantic Partnership Council nations
[c] Mediterranean dialogue country
RAND *MG974-4*

Moreover, non-NATO allies, such as Australia, could rightly argue that they are doing more for the alliance than are key NATO allies. This, too, could lead to an uncomfortable debate about why Australia, for example, appears to be assuming more risks on behalf of the alliance than actual alliance members, such as, say, Germany.

Regardless of how the data are presented to NATO members and their respective publics, NATO heads of state are increasingly finding themselves in a precarious position of explaining to their citizens why, as casualties mount, the mission in Afghanistan is worth the lives lost.

At stake is the possibility of losing not only their political support but also support for the overall mission and the alliance itself.[22]

This debate intensified during 2007. Under intense pressure from opposition parties, Canada's government, led by Prime Minister Stephen Harper, commissioned a review of Canada's commitments. The review concluded that Canada should end its participation unless others did more to share in the risks.[23] In response to Harper, and in an effort to demonstrate greater closeness to NATO, French President Nicholas Sarkozy committed in April 2008 to sending 700 additional French troops to eastern Afghanistan, which in turn would allow American forces to shift troops from the east to the south in support of Canadian forces operating in the vicinity of Kandahar.

The additional French commitment helped alleviate strains on a critical NATO contributor in the short term but fell far short of addressing the more-fundamental long-term issue of risk sharing in the alliance. Those with forces in Afghanistan could well point to other NATO members without forces in Afghanistan and claim that the latter were not sharing equitably in NATO's burdens and risks. But those with forces in the most dangerous areas of Afghanistan could further point to other contributors and noncontributors and claim that the real burdens and risks were being absorbed by the few NATO members suffering mounting casualties. By early 2008, U.S. Secretary of Defense Gates noted: "Some allies ought not to have the luxury of opting for stability and civilian operations, thus forcing other allies to bear a disproportionate share of the fighting and dying." Gates went on to say that NATO had no future as an "alliance of those who are willing to fight and those who are not. Such a development, with all of its implications for collective security, would effectively destroy the

---

[22] While some argue that the Americanization of the war in Afghanistan marks the start of a new effort, others, namely the American public, may disagree. A 2009 poll noted that a majority (51 percent) surveyed believe "the war is not worth the fight." See Steven R. Hurst, "War Weariness in the U.S. Clouds Battle Against Taliban," Associated Press, August 21, 2009.

[23] Government of Canada, Independent Panel on Canada's Future Role in Afghanistan, Ontario, Canada, 2008, pp. 37–38.

alliance."[24] The implications may become evident sooner rather than later as an increasing number of NATO countries plan their exits.[25]

The debate over casualties takes many forms but often surfaces in the debate over national "caveats" (restrictions on the use of forces and equipment) and is a clear manifestation of tensions over who shares in NATO's risks. Caveats have become an ever-increasing source of friction in Afghanistan—and Brussels—as members place specific limitations on what their forces can and cannot do (such as rules for flying at night) with exceptions given only by the member government itself. The Dutch, among others, brought this debate to the forefront early on when they raised the following questions:

> Is this, in fact, not simply a terrorism-fighting mission disguised as a reconstruction effort and thus limited in its capability to act? How much time would the Dutch spend defending themselves against Taliban, drug barons and other militants? And how much time would be left to achieve the stated NATO goal of winning the hearts and minds of the Afghan people?[26]

NATO commanders in Afghanistan continue to express frustration about layers of restrictions and the challenges these restrictions cause when planning and executing operations. During his time as Supreme Allied Commander, General Jones emphatically and openly encouraged governments to decrease the restrictions in an effort to increase the flexibility and capacity of NATO forces. He noted, "the more control a commander has and the more agility he has and the more capability he has is directly related to the number of caveats we have to accomplish the mission."[27] With total force levels in country inadequate to the task, commanders like Jones urged for a relaxation of

---

[24] Ian Traynor, "Allies' Refusal to Boost Afghanistan Troops a Threat to NATO, Gates Says," *The Guardian*, February 11, 2008.

[25] Dutch forces departed in 2010, and Canadian and German forces have announced plans to withdraw in 2011.

[26] Bert Bakker and Lousewies van der Laan, "Why the Netherlands Is Right to Be Wary over Afghanistan," *Financial Times*, February 1, 2006.

[27] J. L. Jones, 2006a.

caveats to maximize the operational capability of available forces and to better address troop shortfalls. Along with shortages, operational risks increase, as Jones emphasized, "you lose one or two infantry battalions, you lose helicopter mobility, you lose reconnaissance capability, you lose some of the critical enablers that you need."[28] As a result, commanders are eager to see restrictions on the activities of their forces removed or to get greater numbers of troops to carry out operations, or preferably both.

Another former NATO commander, General Craddock, spoke of undeclared restrictions and the limitations these restrictions place on ongoing operations. In explaining the matter, Craddock noted, "It's where we're not aware of a situation until [the commander] might ask . . . a nation to move troops to a certain area or conduct a particular task." Craddock went on to note that only then do the restrictions become apparent, and this is often when there is an urgent need for forces or capabilities. Under these circumstances, other contributors must come forward with forces, which disrupts the activity and occasionally breaks habitual relationships, or the command might be forced to forego the operation altogether.[29]

Alternatively, in the absence of such contributors, the combination of caveats and unmet operational needs has left NATO commanders to rely more heavily on available assets to fill the void. Airpower, for example, plays a major role in Afghanistan in support of ground operations because of its ability to target forces and facilities in complex terrain with a high degree of accuracy and precision.

However, heavy reliance on airpower has come at a price. In a counterinsurgency environment where the adversary can blend in with the local population or use innocent civilians as human shields, the risk of civilian casualties will remain a significant concern, as even the most accurate weapons are not accurate 100 percent of the time. Moreover, although all air attacks are directed from the ground, NATO and U.S.

---

[28] Vince Crawley, "NATO's Jones Says Allies Growing More Flexible in Afghanistan," USINFO, U.S. Department of State, November 29, 2006.

[29] Marina Melenic, "Craddock Warns Alliance Credibility Is on the Line in Afghanistan," *Inside the Army*, May 21, 2007.

forces are not always in a position to determine whether claims of civilian casualties are true or not. Given that one of the central objectives of a counterinsurgency campaign is to protect the local population and win its support, the potential for backlash rises when civilian casualties do occur, or are claimed to have occurred, be it from attacks from air or ground forces. Such backlashes have occurred in Afghanistan when incidents involving civilian casualties brought complaints from the Afghan government and UN officials. These strong reactions have forced NATO to rethink not only how to respond to various threats but also its strategy more broadly, given the operational limitations and risks at hand. Indeed, by summer 2009, the new American commander placed severe restrictions on the use of airpower: He was prepared to accept tactical risk except in cases risking "troops in contact."[30]

Limitations on the uses of forces and capabilities, which clearly are an extension of the debate about risks, have placed real constraints on operational commanders—some of which are intended, others are not—and continue to be a major source of friction between NATO's political and military leaders, one that will not be resolved anytime soon. Speaking candidly on the matter of caveats, Craddock observed, "It's probably a lack of forethought as opposed to a Machiavellian desire to muck it up."[31]

Redefining Roles: NATO Members and Nonmembers

Much of the burden-sharing debate stems from the reality that NATO embraced a mission in Afghanistan without a clearly defined strategy and without designating the roles and responsibilities of participating nations. This was not so much an oversight as the consequence of feeling an impetus to act without fully anticipating the wide range

---

[30] See Julian E. Barnes, "U.S. Commander in Afghanistan Shifts Focus to Protecting People," *Los Angeles Times*, July 26, 2009. See also Julian E. Barnes, "Petraeus Takes Over as Head of U.S. Central Command," *Los Angeles Times*, November 1, 2008; Candace Rondeaux, "NATO Modifies Airstrike Policy in Afghanistan," *Washington Post*, October 16, 2008; and Ann Scott Tyson, "Petraeus Mounts Strategy Review," *Washington Post*, October 16, 2008.

[31] Melenic, 2007.

of demands that would fall to the ISAF countries. As a result, even seven years into the mission, the roles and responsibilities of individual NATO members and nonmembers are still not clear and are seemingly decided on a short-term, ad hoc basis.

As discussed in Chapter Four, as operations in Afghanistan began, various ISAF members took on certain tasks, such as training Afghan security forces, leading reconstruction operations, or engaging insurgents and the Taliban in direct military operations. However, on the ground in Afghanistan, military commanders continue to adjust their operations according to the assets available, the operational constraints they face, and the threats they confront. By contrast, NATO heads of state are forced to weigh their levels of commitment, taking into account political pressures, public support, and available resources. In a sense, because of the nature of out-of-area operations, military commanders—both in the field and in Brussels and Mons—occasionally find themselves working at the edges of the political guidance they have received and at odds with their political leaders. Such misalignment between the military and civilian halves of NATO hinders the development of a broader unity of effort and further complicates attempts to establish more clearly defined roles and responsibilities.[32]

These existing divisions feed debates among NATO members and nonmembers about who is doing what, who signed up for what, and who is willing to take on more. Moreover, countries contributing substantial troops and resources to NATO's ISAF mission feel empowered to demand more voice in overall decisions as well as more contributions from partner nations. Canada, for example, has shown considerable willingness to share in the burdens and risk in Afghanistan, which has given Canadian leaders a disproportionately large voice in NATO circles. And this extends far beyond NATO. Australia, although not a member of NATO, is also playing an important role in Afghanistan and seeks a voice in how strategy is developed and operations are car-

---

[32] In January 2010, NATO announced the establishment of a new top civilian post to act as a counterpart to the military chief; however, it remains to be seen whether this position will help align NATO's military and civilian efforts. See Yaroslav Trofimov, "NATO Plans New Top Job in Kabul," *Wall Street Journal*, January 21, 2010.

ried out. As additional non-NATO members continue to participate and lend support, it is not inconceivable that, over time, more will want a greater say. So, while NATO struggles to maintain consensus in the institution, it must also reconcile the role non-NATO members play in exchange for their contributions to the NATO-led operation.

Beyond NATO itself, the role of the EU remains an open question. Given the number of shared members between the two organizations, the EU remains the obvious civilian partner for NATO. However, if the Afghanistan experience is any indication, NATO–EU relations will remain a source of friction,[33] particularly when they involve actual operations and real demands from civil and military elements, as opposed to theoretical constructs of how such a partnership might work.

In the run-up to the April 2008 NATO summit in Bucharest, Romania, more and more attention turned to the enormity of the challenges in Afghanistan. NATO's military commanders noted frequently that military forces can help create security and, therefore, provide "space" for long-term success in Afghanistan, but they cannot by themselves be the recipe for success.[34] And NATO's heads of state emphasized the importance of reconstruction and development as key elements that will lead to long-term success in Afghanistan, although they were looking for others outside NATO to help underwrite the cost. Not surprisingly, some turned to the EU to complement the "hard power" NATO provides. These same voices even called for NATO to explore the possibility of a "Berlin Plus in Reverse," where, rather than enabling NATO assets to be used for EU-led operations,

---

[33] See, for example, Carl Bildt and Anders Fogh Rasmussen, "Don't Discount Europe's Commitment to Afghanistan," *Washington Post*, January 8, 2010.

[34] General Craddock, NATO's now-retired commander, emphasized that "continued success in Afghanistan will not be measured in a military victory." Only a year earlier, his predecessor, General James Jones, had much the same to say: "The key message that I think needs to be delivered for Afghanistan is that Afghanistan's long-term solution is not only a military problem." See Jim Garamone, "Training Afghan Army Remains Key to Stability," American Forces Press Service, October 10, 2007; General James L. Jones, "Update on NATO Operations in Afghanistan," Foreign Press Center Roundtable, Washington, D.C., October 24, 2006b; and Judy Dempsey, "NATO Chief Urges Overhaul of Afghanistan Effort," *International Herald Tribune*, November 5, 2006.

"the EU [would be] coming to the aid of a NATO-led operation with non-military assets and capabilities, on a case-by-case basis."[35] The EU has taken on selected responsibilities in Afghanistan (such as helping to develop the judicial system); however, structural and political concerns, as well as outright limitations in overall capacity, have hampered a greater commitment that NATO leaders desire.[36]

While it seems unlikely the EU will move into the role of filling important capability voids in the near term, NATO leaders should continue to pursue strong NATO–EU links and should focus on expanding overall capacity in key areas, particularly civilian capacity, that can help develop local governing structures. Given France's renewed military connections with NATO, some of the political barriers that separate NATO and the EU could decrease, allowing attention to focus on the development of key civilian capabilities that are in such demand in Afghanistan and will likely remain in high demand for years to come. Other barriers, however, will likely persist because of tensions among other NATO and EU members (e.g., over the role of Turkey, which is a NATO member and long-frustrated EU aspirant). While better NATO–EU relations would help, they should not be seen as a panacea, given the continued tensions that are all too evident in NATO itself.

Additionally, given that ISAF is a UN-mandated force, having the UN in an oversight role could help ease the assignment of tasks in NATO and could diffuse tensions between NATO and the EU. However, the UN has been plagued by its own challenges, preventing it from being able to fully embrace such a role. One measure that would have helped the UN facilitate such a role at the outset was to appoint a special envoy to Afghanistan. The initial proposal for a "triple-hatted" position (helping to coordinate UN, NATO, and EU efforts) eventu-

---

[35] Klaus Naumann, John Shalikashvili, The Lord Inge, Jacques Lanxade, and Henk van den Breemen, *Towards a Grand Strategy for an Uncertain World: Renewing Transatlantic Partnership*, Lunteren, the Netherlands: Noaber Foundation, January 2008.

[36] In August 2009, new NATO Secretary General Anders Fogh Rasmussen reiterated the need for greater assistance from the EU and UN in Afghanistan. See Secretary General Anders Fogh Rasmussen, "First NATO Press Conference," transcript, August 3, 2009. Also, for example, see Judy Dempsey, "EU and NATO Bound in Perilous Rivalry," *International Herald Tribune*, October 4, 2006.

ally collapsed, with the various parties eventually agreeing on a more-limited role. Even so, Ambassador Kai Eide, the first UN Special Representative in Afghanistan, was only appointed in March 2008.[37] The extent to which Ambassador Eide was successful in breaking down some of the existing barriers (between NATO, the UN, the EU, and the Afghan government) remains to be seen.[38] If it remains likely that NATO will continue to conduct such out-of-area security operations, discussions and decisions on roles and responsibilities for all key parties—NATO, the EU, and the UN—should take place from the outset to avoid NATO's current predicament of acting first and organizing later.

While more productive NATO–EU, NATO–UN, and NATO–EU–UN relations need to be part of the alliance's longer-term goals, NATO leaders need to beware the temptation of making any lack of progress in building these relations the scapegoat for NATO failures in Afghanistan. Seeking cooperation with entities that can help with governance and reconstruction in Afghanistan will be important to NATO's success, but NATO leaders also need to recall that it was NATO, not the EU or the UN, that accepted responsibilities in Afghanistan. Therefore, it will be NATO leadership that will be essential to work toward more promising outcomes.

Managing Expectations—From Summits on Down

During a period of less than 18 months, two NATO summits provided NATO heads of state opportunities not only to clarify the alliance's role in Afghanistan but also to reconfirm its commitment to the mission.[39] Prior to each summit, the heads of state were asked to reconfirm their commitment to the mission in Afghanistan, pledge greater

---

[37] Ambassador Eide stepped down in March 2010 and was replaced by Staffan de Mistura.

[38] Indeed, many may instead relate his term to the controversy surrounding the 2009 Afghan elections and his dispute with the UN deputy special representative to Afghanistan, Peter Galbraith, which ultimately lead to Galbraith's firing.

[39] The Riga Summit took place in November 2006, and the Bucharest Summit in April 2008.

resources to the ongoing effort there, and consider relaxing or eliminating restrictions on forces. Each summit produced a communiqué that was supportive in tone but accompanied by relatively little action.[40]

For example, prior to the November 2006 Riga Summit, General Jones pressed allied leaders, noting that "Removing caveats is tantamount to raising more forces."[41] Jones received little in return. At the same time, other leaders were making a concerted effort to diffuse tensions over caveats prior to the summit. As Germany's Chancellor Angela Merkel noted, "The issue of Afghanistan is too important for us to let it be reduced to a military north-south debate."[42] Merkel's comments were hardly satisfying to the NATO and non-NATO allies bearing the brunt of the fighting in the volatile south and east.

Still others have tried to change the character of the ongoing NATO debate. Then–NATO Secretary General De Hoop Scheffer emphasized the need for NATO to adapt as an alliance to address threats that may originate from afar. In his words, "Either we tackle these problems when and where they emerge, or they will end up on our doorstep."[43]

During both summits, NATO heads of state clearly understood that NATO was in for a hard fight in Afghanistan and remained optimistic about succeeding. But they were only prepared to act incrementally to address the most pressing problems. Each time, the heads of state spoke in optimistic terms but found themselves constrained politically from taking further action. Secretary General De Hoop Scheffer's comment at the conclusion of the Riga Summit is illustrative: "It's winnable. It's being won, but not yet won."[44]

---

[40] See North Atlantic Council, "Riga Summit Declaration," Riga, Latvia, November 29, 2006.

[41] Paul Ames, "NATO Commander Seeking Strengthening of Afghan Force Ahead of Key Summit," Associated Press, November 22, 2006.

[42] "Merkel Rules Out German Role in Volatile Southern Afghanistan," Agence France Presse, November 22, 2006.

[43] Jaap de Hoop Scheffer, "Reflections on the Riga Summit," NATO Review, Winter 2006b.

[44] Jaap de Hoop Scheffer, "Closing Press Conference," Riga, Latvia, November 29, 2006a.

What NATO leaders have not yet confronted, at least not in their public statements, is whether NATO has the staying power to achieve long-term success in Afghanistan. A series of reports in early 2008—including one led by retired General Jones—called for renewed attention on the growing challenges posed in Afghanistan and noted that, even as the situation in Iraq appeared (at least for the time being) to be stabilizing, the situation in Afghanistan was deteriorating sharply. The intent of the reports was clear: to intensify the focus on Afghanistan and to bring additional pressure on NATO leaders to produce a more-cohesive strategy and a more-viable set of commitments at the Bucharest summit.[45] The reports' influence, however, was fleeting; the various recommendations seemed to fade from view almost as quickly as they were introduced.

It is perhaps telling that, even during NATO's 60th anniversary celebrations in Strasbourg, France, and Kehl, Germany, in April 2009, calls for additional resources to support operations in Afghanistan were noticeably absent.[46] Instead, the discussion on Afghanistan focused on the growing U.S. role and the start of a "strategic review of U.S. policy in the Afghanistan/Pakistan region that will serve as a basis for discussions on the future direction of ISAF."[47] Additionally, both U.S. and NATO officials emphasized the training mission as an opportunity for NATO members to do more, in concert with the announcement of the formation of NTM-A.[48] Nevertheless, the seeming absence of a debate on operations in Afghanistan, despite rising casualties and continued Taliban threat, revealed the heightened sensitivities in NATO and the

---

[45] Afghanistan Study Group, *Revitalizing Our Efforts, Rethinking Our Strategies*, 2nd ed., Washington, D.C.: Center for the Study of the Presidency, January 30, 2008; Atlantic Council of the United States, "Saving Afghanistan: An Appeal and Plan for Urgent Action," issue brief, Washington, D.C., January 28, 2008; International Crisis Group, "Afghanistan: The Need for International Resolve," Washington, D.C., Asia Report 145, February 6, 2008.

[46] Paul Belkin, Carl Ek, Lisa Mages, and Derek E. Mix, "NATO's 60th Anniversary Summit," Washington, D.C.: Congressional Research Service, April 14, 2009, p. 4.

[47] Belkin et al., 2009, p. 2.

[48] The purpose of the NTM-A is to provide senior-level mentoring and training to ANA and ANP. For more details, please see Belkin et al., 2009; NATO, "Fact Sheet: NATO Training Mission—Afghanistan (NTM-A)," October 2009c; and NATO, 2010a.

extent to which negative discussions from the NATO leadership had the potential to adversely affect the mission.

Even at the London Conference in January 2010, NATO members emphasized the criticality of the training mission, but many have yet to make good on pledges for funding and troops.[49] While NATO members seem increasingly focused on transferring responsibilities back to the Afghans (particularly ANSF) to enable their own forces to come home,[50] they remain hesitant to provide the resources to meet stated goals and time lines. In a sense, perhaps one ramification of the Americanization of the effort has led some NATO members to feel less pressure to contribute: Acting in support of the alliance is different from acting in support of the United States. Perhaps tellingly, after announcing Germany would only contribute 500 additional troops (compared to hopes of 1,500 more) and would begin withdrawing in 2011, Chancellor Angela Merkel stated, "We have nothing to be ashamed of . . . It was not the case that the Americans asked us what we wanted to do, but rather we determined ourselves what we intend to do."[51]

Additionally, part of NATO's reluctance to demonstrate the staying power needed to succeed in Afghanistan may be attributable to a gradual but steady erosion of confidence in Afghanistan's national leaders. After a fairly lengthy period of support for the Karzai leadership, concern mounted not merely about corruption generally in Afghanistan but about corruption extending to the highest levels of the Karzai government. By the latter half of 2006, the concern was being expressed openly and has not receded since.[52] Suggestions that Afghan authorities, particularly the Afghan police, have been openly collaborating with the Taliban have fueled speculation that Karzai's government is not capable of controlling—to say nothing of disciplining—its own leaders. Evidence that local police authorities

---

[49] Whitlock, 2010.

[50] See Anders Fogh Rasmussen, "A New Momentum for Afghanistan," *Washington Post*, December 4, 2009.

[51] Whitlock, 2010.

[52] See, for example, Carlotta Gall, "Doubts About Karzai Growing," *International Herald Tribune*, August 22, 2006.

may have collaborated with the Taliban in 2008 to target American forces greatly fueled these concerns.[53] Indeed, by 2009, Secretary General Scheffer stated: "The basic problem in Afghanistan is not too much Taliban; it's too little good governance."[54]

Nevertheless, despite the unease with Karzai, it is not clear that there is a viable alternative. Although NATO received Karzai publicly at the Bucharest summit, considerable unease remains about his leadership, particularly among the British. The 2009 Afghan elections further highlighted this tension, as Karzai remained in power following a controversial election widely perceived as deeply flawed. The election showed the effects a lack of confidence in Karzai's government could have on NATO's staying power. As one report noted following the London Conference,

> The elephant in the room at yesterday's conference was just how much longer the West is prepared to risk the lives of its soldiers for a cause that many of their countrymen no longer believe in, or are prepared to support.[55]

Pakistan remains the other obstacle to success. As time passed, NATO leaders came to understand that they could not deal effectively with the security problems inside Afghanistan without addressing the security threats emanating from Pakistan. When NATO's responsibilities were limited to Kabul and the northern parts of Afghanistan, NATO leaders generally could assume away the challenges emanating from Pakistan as an American problem. But as NATO's responsibilities expanded and as the Taliban threat, which was being organized and supported from Pakistani territory, grew in numbers and sophistication, NATO leaders could no longer wish the problem away. Recognizing the problem did not, however, lead to a solution. NATO had

---

[53] See Eric Schmitt, "Afghan Officials Aided Attack on U.S. Soldiers," *New York Times*, November 3, 2008.

[54] Jaap de Hoop Scheffer, "Afghanistan: We Can Do Better," *Washington Post*, January 18, 2009.

[55] Con Coughlin, "Has the West Got the Will to Carry on Shedding Blood for the Afghans?" *Daily Telegraph* (London), January 29, 2010.

little or no experience in dealing with Pakistan, and strong and consistent voices in NATO resisted further expansion of NATO's mission. Although some saw it necessary to engage Pakistan diplomatically, most feared that NATO could find itself pitted against Pakistani forces over disputed border areas. Several NATO members, particularly the British and Americans, seemed doubtful that NATO could help with Pakistan, and therefore cautioned against any further involvement. The Americans, in the meantime, continue to target militants in Pakistan's tribal region by using drones controlled by the Central Intelligence Agency.[56]

Still, NATO leaders understand that the alliance runs real risks with Pakistan and that, if support for the Taliban inside Pakistan cannot be tempered, the prospect of military clashes will continue to grow and could ultimately include threats to NATO supply lines that run through Pakistan, as is now the case. This has a bearing not only on broad NATO support for the mission but also on NATO members' willingness to commit forces to the most dangerous areas of Afghanistan for fear that national forces, under NATO command, might become engaged directly with Pakistani-supported forces or, worse, Pakistan's army.

Most NATO leaders understand that a political solution in Afghanistan will require some level of reconciliation with the Taliban, many of whom reside in Pakistan.[57] Reaching out to Taliban members, across the border into Pakistan, will necessitate delicate diplomatic maneuvering that will be nearly impossible without some form of political dialogue with Pakistani officials.[58] NATO leaders may be content that British and American leaders orchestrate such contacts through national channels, but it is likely that, at some point, NATO

---

[56] Eric Schmitt and Christopher Drew, "More Drone Attacks in Pakistan Planned," *New York Times*, April 6, 2009.

[57] Although many agree that reconciliation or a negotiated settlement are necessary, disagreement remains about when this should occur. See James Dobbins, "Talking to the Taliban," *New York Times*, May 11, 2010.

[58] Jane Perlez, "Pakistan Is Said to Pursue Role in U.S.-Afghan Talks," *New York Times*, February 9, 2010.

itself will want to establish some form of political channel to Pakistani leaders, if only to facilitate contact with Taliban elements living and operating from inside Pakistan.

Just as NATO leaders contemplate how commitments can be sustained, they also are being forced to contemplate how commitments are being managed. Now, after seven years of involvement in Afghanistan, NATO has yet to draw on any of its existing headquarters structures to command forces in the operation and has ruled out the option of committing any "standing" forces or capabilities to the operation. Even the recently created NRF, which was established in many ways to contend with circumstances like Afghanistan, has been kept off the roster of available forces. Instead, NATO countries have chosen to draw on forces for Afghanistan that fall outside their normal NATO commitments, working with a set of ad hoc command arrangements and ad hoc force commitments, many of which are made in piecemeal fashion.

A likely result could be the emergence of "two NATOs" or, at the very least, two distinctly different levels of experience in NATO: first, the cadre of experienced forces that have participated in operations in Afghanistan and have brought important lessons back to their home countries and to the alliance as a whole but that are not part of standing NATO structures, and second, the standing command structure and regularly assigned forces that have not been called on to help with what arguably is one of NATO's most important missions to date and have not benefited from recent battle experience. Time will tell whether this has lasting effects on the alliance, but there is little question that NATO has made a tremendous investment in standing structures and processes to generate a formal commitment of forces that have not been called on thus far to contribute to the mission in Afghanistan and that cannot rightly be called "battle tested" in comparison with the forces that have served there. This might also call into question the need for many of the standing headquarters and standing force commitments, particularly the NRF.

Ultimately, as the security situation in Afghanistan remains highly challenging or perhaps deteriorates further, as the costs for reconstruction and development grow, and as the politics in Afghanistan become more difficult to navigate,[59] the challenges and costs for NATO will only expand. There is little likelihood that the situation in Afghanistan will stabilize in the short term, and there is every reason to believe that NATO will be involved in Afghanistan for the long term. While frictions in the alliance have been managed thus far, and indeed relations in the alliance are far better than they were just a few years ago, we should expect tensions to mount, particularly if improvements to the security situation prove elusive and casualties grow. Just as America's war in Iraq produced a domestic backlash in American politics, particularly when the security situation there looked dire, it is reasonable to assume that NATO's long war in Afghanistan may produce a backlash in NATO polities.

As in its earlier history, there are good reasons to believe that NATO, through a series of successive albeit incremental steps, will adapt to the changing circumstances in Afghanistan and maintain support for the overall effort. These steps may include increased resources (such as troops, trainers, equipment, and financial aid), a renewed commitment in support of NATO's role in Afghanistan, or relaxed caveats on forces currently assisting with operations. Certainly, these are not the only steps that can be taken, but they serve as examples of ways NATO members can reconfirm their commitment and support not only to NATO as an alliance but also to completing and succeeding at its mission in Afghanistan. What will ultimately undermine support, however, is if casualties mount—including civilian casualties among NATO partners and inside Afghanistan and even Pakistan—and the burdens of those losses are shared unequally among NATO's partners. This is not an experience that NATO has endured before, and it is not clear that it is one that can be readily managed. There certainly is little indication that NATO heads of state have taken steps to manage such an eventuality.

---

[59] More than a few careful observers have cautioned that President Karzai maintains tenuous control at best and that his influence is highly constrained beyond the immediate reaches of Kabul. See, for example, Eric Schmitt, "U.S. Envoy's Cables Show Worries on Afghan Plans," *New York Times*, January 25, 2010.

CHAPTER SIX

What Might Be Next for NATO?

We are on the edge of a precipice.

—Lord George Robertson, 2010[1]

The changing character of the NATO alliance since the late days of the Cold War has been a story of endurance and adaptability. Looking back over what is now more than 20 years, it was never certain that the alliance would remain intact; that its membership would expand, not just once but three times; and that it would commit itself to operations outside the geographic area of the alliance on three separate occasions. It is far too easy to declare each new challenge NATO confronts as a defining moment for the alliance. Surely, as Operation Allied Force wound down in summer 1999, few if any observers would have expected NATO to be involved again, in just a few short years, in far-off Afghanistan. Indeed, many saw Allied Force as the outer limit of NATO's out-of-area operations, with the strains on the alliance too great to contemplate anything seemingly so ambitious for many years to come. This clearly was the view of Bush administration, with its emphasis on coalitions of the willing.[2] Yet counting NATO out, as some are inclined to do, seems exaggerated and misplaced.[3] That does

---

[1] Lord George Robertson is the former Secretary General of NATO and spoke on the challenges facing the alliance. See George Robertson, "The Transatlantic Community: Time for Some Lateral Thinking," Washington, D.C.: Atlantic Council, March 2, 2010.

[2] See Chapter Three for more on coalitions of the willing.

[3] See Bacevich, 2008.

not mean NATO will escape a lengthy period of retrenchment and introspection, leading to the obvious question: What might be next for NATO?

For an alliance that seemed desperate to act, to demonstrate that it could do *something* in the aftermath of 9/11, it is now in the position of being responsible for doing everything in Afghanistan. Despite the caveats and restrictions, despite insufficient troops and equipment, despite ever-growing threats and resurgent attacks from enemy forces, and despite a general uneasiness among NATO's political leaders and their publics, NATO troops have thus far performed reasonably well, given the difficulties of operating at such a distance and with the constraints on NATO's military leaders. Although NATO's mission in Afghanistan continues to be under enormous strain and although the alliance will likely be committed there for many years to come, the direst of predictions have not played out. NATO may yet confront far more trying circumstances in Afghanistan or in response to instability in neighboring Pakistan, and tensions in the alliance could peak. This increase in tension could fragment the alliance, with some members staying and others departing, or the alliance as a whole might choose to end its commitment in Afghanistan, leaving the United States and whatever other countries choose to remain to form a new partnership. Moreover, the problems Afghanistan presents need not become vastly more difficult before many NATO members tire,[4] spurring a debate among NATO's leaders and their publics to end its commitment.

Indeed, in some form or another, this outcome appears increasingly likely: Afghanistan remains a NATO operation in name only, with fewer and fewer NATO members contributing actively to ISAF operations. For that matter, there is no escaping that the "Americanization" of the Afghanistan commitment, which began in 2008 but which became pronounced in 2009 and 2010, could likely prove to

---

[4]   By June 2009, U.S. Secretary of Defense Gates was issuing warnings that time was short in Afghanistan. Even the new U.S. administration, which came to office in early 2009 committed to rededicating itself to the mission in Afghanistan, recognized that its commitment could not be indefinite. See Julian E. Barnes, "Gates Open to Sending More Troops to Afghanistan," *Los Angeles Times*, September 4, 2009; Gordon Lubold, "In Afghanistan, Time Is Running Out, Pentagon Worries," *Christian Science Monitor*, June 2, 2009.

be positive for Afghanistan but ultimately negative for NATO. Thus, Americans assuming much more of the risk does not leave NATO in any better place and does not leave NATO off the hook. It does relieve NATO of some of the burdens and risks but, in turn, makes NATO the junior partner.[5] As a result, Afghanistan may no longer be viewed as an alliance mission but as a U.S. mission with key NATO contributions.

Any future successes in Afghanistan will be credited to the second American "surge"[6] and not to a newfound sense of NATO unity and resilience. American policymakers will be sure to credit NATO for its many contributions when the circumstances demand it, but they will not be quick to forget that NATO seemed incapable of marshaling what was necessary to succeed in the first place and unable to recapture momentum once it was lost.[7] For their part, NATO's European leaders will readily accept any accolades offered but will not soon forget how outmatched they seemed to be when it came time to make good on NATO's commitments in Afghanistan.

Recognizing this reality, however harsh, would offer a fresh point of departure for NATO heads of state and might begin to help answer the question about what is next for NATO. The effort needs to begin with a more coordinated effort by NATO heads of state to manage expectations among NATO members and their respective publics. American leaders need to recognize that NATO has little more to give, and NATO's European leaders need to accept (and appreciate) that the United States has once again stepped in to fill the void, that NATO is now supporting an American-led effort. Addressing the misalignment in expectations will help establish a new reality for NATO and will aid the development of a more-holistic long-term strategy for Afghanistan. This, in turn, could help NATO prove its resiliency as an alliance and institution.

---

[5] The irony here is that former President George W. Bush was willing to treat NATO as an equal partner.

[6] The first "surge," of course, occurred in Iraq beginning in late 2006.

[7] See Vinocur, 2009.

Accepting a new reality does not mean that NATO can completely opt out of Afghanistan or merely allow its commitment to wither on the vine. Even in a significantly reduced role in support of an American-led effort, NATO leaders need to dedicate more political attention to reaching a consensus on the definition of success. This, in turn, will require NATO's political and military leaders to coordinate the level of demands, commitment, and resources required to complete the mission. Establishing such a baseline will thereby enable commanders on the ground and heads of state back home to work together to address any imbalance existing across the alliance—in terms of troop levels, funding, and equipment—and will also foster greater cohesion of NATO efforts.

To date, the highly fragile security situation in Afghanistan has perhaps drawn far too much attention to the debate over how many and what kinds of troops and equipment NATO will commit to operations in Afghanistan and too little attention to NATO's ability to create a viable Afghan security force. It is the latter, however, that is most crucial for NATO's (and America's) exit strategy and for long-term stability. While debates about whether or not various NATO members are meeting their responsibilities to provide troops and equipment are important, so too are debates about what is necessary to train, equip, and support Afghan security forces adequately. NATO has fallen considerably short of providing the training expertise to create a viable Afghan security force,[8] to say nothing of investments in other critical governing structures.

Here is an area in which the beginnings of a new reality might be forged. NATO is unlikely to take up any more of the combat functions in Afghanistan. Indeed, its relative role has declined considerably in recent months. But NATO partners could assume a greater role in training and expanding Afghan security forces. NATO leaders, particularly American leaders, will need to work hard to avoid the inevitable

---

[8]   By one estimate, NATO is short 1,500 to 1,700 instructors or trainers and approximately 2,500 mentors in Afghanistan from the total deemed necessary to meet the stated goals and time line for developing the Afghan national security forces. See Adam Entous, "US Makes Appeal to NATO on Afghan Training," Reuters, February 4, 2010. We also recognize that U.S. forces under OEF are also in need of more military trainers (see Chapter Four).

shorthand that "NATO trains while America fights," but such a new set of arrangements might point to a more-viable partnership. It would recognize not only that there are limits to what NATO's European partners can contribute but would also remedy an important short-coming in the American- and NATO-led efforts to date. Implementing such a step would likely benefit by establishing an ISAF training command under a European-led commander.

Should the renewed American focus on gaining and maintaining stability in key regions bear fruit over the next 12 to 18 months and should a more-concerted NATO effort begin to produce more robust and more capable ANSF, the United States and NATO could get past the era of finger-pointing over who lost Afghanistan and in turn look to the moment when the transatlantic partnership began to yield measurable success. Over time, significant increases in Afghan security capabilities would allow NATO's European partners and the United States to scale back on their respective commitments of troops and materiel. It would also place the NATO-Afghanistan relationship on a much more stable footing for the long term, since the Afghan government would be much less dependent on NATO and U.S. forces to meet its basic security needs.

This is not meant to imply that, should a new reality be forged that focuses on NATO's training responsibilities and should such arrangements succeed, NATO has entered a new era. Afghanistan will continue to challenge the alliance in a host of ways, some anticipated and many not. A NATO training focus in Afghanistan would not naturally suggest a NATO training focus in other challenging areas of the globe. The Afghanistan experience has almost certainly tested the limits of NATO's ambitions and reach for a long time to come.

Furthermore, although there is, or perhaps was, a temptation among some NATO members to look beyond Afghanistan and think of a future in which NATO serves as the basis for a global alliance or for tackling initiatives globally,[9] which might include the likes of

---

[9]   See, for example, Zbigniew Brzezinski, "An Agenda for NATO: Toward a Global Security Web," *Foreign Affairs*, September/October 2009. Additionally, advocates of this view saw former Prime Minister Shinzo Abe's January 2007 visit to NATO as a hopeful sign. See

Japan, Australia, and South Korea, that path could prove to be difficult if not impossible to navigate. NATO no longer appears to have an appetite for such a venture—if, in fact, it ever did—and the list of potential partners may be approaching zero.[10] What is far more likely is that NATO members will conclude that their problems closer to home are growing in importance and sophistication and that NATO's key members—perhaps including the United States—lack the will to become entangled in anything nearly as challenging as the Afghanistan commitment has proven to be.

For the future, NATO's attention will almost certainly turn to problems closer to home, such as confronting the continuing threat of radical Islam in the Middle East and the burgeoning Islamic population inside Europe, dealing with problems of piracy along NATO's periphery, and perhaps contending with the emerging threat of Iran's ambition for nuclear weapons. NATO will want to continue to interact with Russia in constructive ways, but some NATO members, particularly the new NATO members, will always be wary of Russia's intentions and will point to Russian provocations with a certain level of alarm, especially after Russia's August 2008 military intervention in Georgia.[11] Russia, in turn, will continue to test NATO, with the aim of stressing or even fracturing NATO solidarity, on a range of matters along its periphery. Russia will be particularly meddlesome when it comes to considering new members of the alliance, significantly raising the cost of entry for such new members as Georgia and Ukraine. NATO could feel compelled to play a larger security role in sub-Saharan Africa, although to date the alliance has shown little appetite

---

"Abe's Visit to Europe Has Great Significance," *The Daily Yomiuri*, January 10, 2007. Still others, outside NATO circles, viewed NATO's outreach with some suspicion, as motivated perhaps by a need for troops and resources more than by a desire to create a global institution.

[10] Germany's General (retired) Klaus Naumann's recent sentiments—"the alliance should not be made into a global actor"—are indicative of such a view. See Naumann, 2009, p. 62.

[11] Ian Traynor, "Russia Accused of Unleashing Cyberwar to Disable Estonia: Parliament, Ministries, Banks, Media Targeted: NATO Experts Sent in to Strengthen Defences," *The Guardian*, May 17, 2007; NATO, "NATO Foreign Ministers Reiterate Support for Georgia," *North Atlantic Treaty Organization News*, August 20, 2008.

to get involved there; nor for that matter do the African states seem eager for greater NATO involvement.

NATO's 60th anniversary, commemorated in spring 2009, provided NATO's leaders an opportunity to reflect on the future of the alliance and chart future directions. By all indications, the anniversary focused more on past glory than on future opportunities and thus proved to be a missed opportunity, perhaps because the strains on the alliance were simply too fresh to be considered with any perspective. After more than seven years of continuous involvement in Afghanistan, there is no doubt that some NATO leaders would prefer that NATO "come home" to Europe, particularly given the unsettled relationships that surround much of NATO's periphery. Others certainly sympathize with earlier admonitions that NATO's future is "out of area or out of business" but now do so from a much more cautious position than those who first gave voice to the position. Those responsible for crafting messages on NATO's future strategic directions will likely want to capture both points of view: NATO does have important responsibilities at home, and NATO will want to remain involved in the world beyond its immediate area of responsibility, if for no other reason than the rest of the world will not likely let NATO retreat to the comfortable confines of Europe. The initial draft of a new strategic concept for NATO will undoubtedly capture these themes while struggling to show a renewed emphasis on NATO's role in Afghanistan.[12]

It is conceivable that NATO might want to establish a set of guidelines, if only informal guidelines, revalidating core commitments and governing future commitments and the use of force.[13] Indeed, the

---

[12] See Christopher S. Chivvis, "Recasting NATO's Strategic Concept: Possible Directions for the United States," Santa Monica, Calif.: RAND Corporation, OP-280-AF, 2009. The new NATO Strategic Concept is anticipated to be released at the fall 2010 NATO summit to be held in Lisbon.

[13] This would be reminiscent of the American debate in the mid-1980s, when Secretary of State George Shultz and Secretary of Defense Caspar Weinberger established competing guidelines that would govern commitment of American troops. Shultz's guidelines tended to be more permissive, while Weinberger's were far more restrictive. See Richard Halloran, "Shultz and Weinberger: Disputing Use of Force," *New York Times*, November 30, 1984. Additionally, we acknowledge the May 2010 report by a group of experts (chaired by Madeleine K. Albright), which also discussed establishing guidelines for future missions. See

effort to develop a strategic concept may present an opportunity to develop these guidelines in a way that adequately captures the current security environment and threats to NATO members. Such guidelines would undoubtedly include the following parameters:

- **Individual member countries:** Is there strong political support of any new commitments from the outset?
  - Has there been active public outreach, including a discussion of what the mission may entail, including the risk of casualties?
- **Internal NATO:** Is there a willingness and readiness to adapt to changing circumstances?
  - How flexible is the alliance? What limitations and mission constraints currently exist or may arise (e.g., other NATO missions)?
- **NATO and non-NATO members:** Is there clarity of roles among NATO and non-NATO members?
  - Are capabilities matched to the mission?

Any NATO discussions on the use of force require a balance between diplomatic and military power. Debates on these issues should therefore not be undertaken inside military channels only. This responsibility might be more suitable for NATO heads of state or a senior-level working body (i.e., the executive working group). Regardless of whether the revised strategic concept tackles the governing rules of engagement or whether it is decided by another NATO body, the effort itself would aid NATO in understanding the constraints, limitations, and potential breaking points of missions under consideration. Furthermore, this would also present an appropriate forum for addressing external factors that may affect NATO's calculus.[14]

Some might inevitably see such guidelines as applying a set of rules that could never be met—setting the bar so high that NATO

NATO Group of Experts, "NATO 2020: Assured Security; Dynamic Engagement," Brussels: NATO Public Diplomacy Division, May 17, 2010.

[14] In his 2010 speech, Lord Robertson quoted Leon Trotsky when discussing NATO's role in Afghanistan: "We may not be interested in this war, but this war is interested in us." See Robertson, 2010.

could never jump over it. Indeed, there are likely to be some among NATO's ranks who would welcome just such a test. But an informal set of guidelines that could be used to better align NATO political support with anticipated future missions might help avoid the types of risks that NATO might reasonably have anticipated when it first became involved in Afghanistan and when it later assumed a much greater set of responsibilities. At the very least, an informal set of guidelines could give structure to an internal NATO debate that would precede any new formal commitment. Moreover, this could also serve as a guide for reinforcing NATO's commitment once the mission is under way.[15] This type of debate would also help insulate NATO from future detractors, who, as in the Afghanistan experience, could point to the lack of formal debate as a reason for curtailing or pulling back from any future commitment. In this way, the guidelines would not have to be seen as setting a high bar but instead could be seen as the basic point of entry for any new commitment. It clearly would be a reflection of the difficult lessons that NATO has learned from the Afghanistan experience.

Whatever the outcome in Afghanistan, and whether or not NATO chooses to adopt a set of guidelines, it seems reasonably clear that the alliance will not enter any new commitments lightly—perhaps including commitments to new members, such as Georgia and Ukraine—and might well for a time focus on shoring up relationships in the alliance before taking on new responsibilities beyond the North Atlantic area. This is not to presume that NATO's importance on a global scale will be any less; NATO is, and will continue to be, an important global security alliance. For the time being, however, the scope of NATO's future roles abroad may be more limited, such as focusing on humanitarian assistance or training, advising, and assisting nations that seek

---

[15] Here, we are reminded of NATO's campaign in Kosovo and the parallel public diplomacy effort. Lord Robertson noted that the UK Ministry of Defense held a daily press conference, followed by a NATO press conference in the afternoon, and one by the U.S. Department of Defense in the evening. The result of these conferences was that "publics right across the world got the message that we meant business and that we were absolutely committed to achieving our objectives." Such a coordinated and consistent effort could be beneficial for strengthening NATO cohesion. See Robertson, 2010.

support. While these efforts may entail long-term commitments, they would fall well short of committing combat forces. Nevertheless, such missions would require NATO to assess and identify capabilities and skills inherent among its members to determine how they can best contribute to achieve a sustainable and successful effort. But following through on these commitments will be key and will require NATO leaders and their respective publics to understand and support the need to participate in the effort. To the extent that Afghanistan is seen as risking NATO itself, which from this vantage point is hard to escape, most of the allies will be highly reluctant to take up new risks that are not seen as responding to a direct threat to the alliance and its members. The alliance's new strategic concept will undoubtedly seek to balance NATO's various roles at home and abroad, but there should be little doubt that, for the time being, NATO's focus will be at home. The away games appear to be beyond NATO's reach.

Bibliography

"Abe's Visit to Europe Has Great Significance," *The Daily Yomiuri*, January 10, 2007.

Acheson, Dean, *Present at the Creation*, New York: Norton and Company, 1969.

"Afghanistan: Gates Doubts Europeans' War Commitment," *New York Times*, October 26, 2007.

"Afghanistan: NATO Chief Not Ruling Out More Alliance Involvement," Radio Free Europe/Radio Liberty, October 13, 2004.

Afghanistan Study Group, *Revitalizing Our Efforts, Rethinking Our Strategies*, 2nd ed., Washington, D.C.: Center for the Study of the Presidency, January 30, 2008.

Agreement on Provisional Arrangements in Afghanistan Pending the Re-Establishment of Permanent Government Institutions, Bonn, Germany, December 5, 2001. As of June 15, 2010: http://www.un.org/News/dh/latest/afghan/afghan-agree.htm

Ames, Paul, "NATO Commander Seeking Strengthening of Afghan Force Ahead of Key Summit," Associated Press, November 22, 2006.

Asmus, Ronald D., *Opening NATO's Door*, New York: Columbia University Press, 2002.

Atlantic Council of the United States, "Saving Afghanistan: An Appeal and Plan for Urgent Action," issue brief, Washington, D.C., January 28, 2008.

Bacevich, Andrew J., "NATO at Twilight," *Los Angeles Times*, February 11, 2008.

Baker, Gerard, "NATO Is Not Dead but Missing in Action," *Financial Times*, November 21, 2002.

Baker, Luke, and Andrew Quinn, "NATO Allies Offer 7,000 Extra Troops for Afghan War," Reuters, December 4, 2009. As of June 18, 2010: http://www.reuters.com/article/idUSTRE5B31NW20091204

Bakker, Bert, and Lousewies van der Laan, "Why the Netherlands Is Right to Be Wary over Afghanistan," *Financial Times*, February 1, 2006.

Barnes, John F., "Afghan Officials Say Airstrike Killed Civilians," *New York Times*, October 16, 2008.

Barnes, Julian E., "Petraeus Takes Over as Head of U.S. Central Command," *Los Angeles Times*, November 1, 2008.

———, "U.S. Commander in Afghanistan Shifts Focus to Protecting People," *Los Angeles Times*, July 26, 2009.

———, "Gates Open to Sending More Troops to Afghanistan," *Los Angeles Times*, September 4, 2009.

Barno, Lt Gen David W., testimony before the Senate Armed Services Committee, Washington, D.C., February 26, 2009.

Belkin, Paul, Carl Ek, Lisa Mages, and Derek E. Mix, "NATO's 60th Anniversary Summit," Washington, D.C.: Congressional Research Service, April 14, 2009.

Bensahel, Nora, "Separable But Not Separate Forces: NATO's Development of the Combined Joint Task Force," *European Security*, Vol. 8, No. 2, Summer 1999, pp. 52–72.

———, *The Counterterror Coalitions: Cooperation with Europe, NATO, and the European Union*, Santa Monica, Calif.: RAND Corporation, MR-1746-AF, 2003. As of June 16, 2010:
http://www.rand.org/pubs/monograph_reports/MR1746/

Bildt, Carl, and Anders Fogh Rasmussen, "Don't Discount Europe's Commitment to Afghanistan," *Washington Post*, January 8, 2010.

Bilefsky, Dan, "Europe Asked to Send Afghanistan More Troops," *New York Times*, October 8, 2008.

Black, Ian, "NATO Emerges from Bunker with New Role in Afghanistan," *The Guardian*, November 15, 2002.

Bowman, Tom, "U.S. Military Falls Short of Afghan Training Goals," *All Things Considered*, National Public Radio, January 25, 2008.

Bremner, Charles, "Paris and Berlin Prepare Alliance to Rival NATO," *The Times* (London), April 28, 2003.

Brzezinski, Zbigniew, "An Agenda for NATO: Toward a Global Security Web," *Foreign Affairs*, September/October 2009.

Burns, Nicholas, "Transforming NATO's Role," *Boston Globe*, December 22, 2003.

Burns, Robert, "U.S. Commits to Adding Troops to Afghanistan," Associated Press, April 9, 2008.

———, "Pentagon May Beef Up Afghanistan Command Role," Associated Press, May 1, 2008.

Bush, George W., "Address to a Joint Session of Congress and the American People," Washington, D.C.: The White House, Office of the Press Secretary, September 20, 2001. As of June 16, 2010:
http://georgewbush-whitehouse.archives.gov/news/releases/2001/09/20010920-8.html

————, "Presidential Address to the Nation," transcript, Washington, D.C.: The White House, Office of the Press Secretary, October 7, 2001. As of June 16, 2010:
http://georgewbush-whitehouse.archives.gov/news/releases/2001/10/20011007-8.html

————, "President Discusses Homeland Security, Economy with Cabinet," Washington, D.C.: Office of the Press Secretary, November 13, 2002. As of June 16, 2010:
http://www.dhs.gov/xnews/speeches/speech_0019.shtm

————, "President Bush Previews Historic NATO Summit in Prague Speech: Remarks by the President to Prague Atlantic Student Summit," Prague, Czech Republic, November 20, 2002. Online at:
http://georgewbush-whitehouse.archives.gov/news/releases/2002/11/print/20021120-4.html

Byman, Daniel L., and Matthew C. Waxman, "Kosovo and the Great Air Power Debate," *International Security*, Vol. 24, No. 4, Spring 2000, pp. 5–38.

Byman, Daniel L., Matthew C. Waxman, and Eric Larson, *Air Power as a Coercive Instrument*, Santa Monica, Calif.: RAND Corporation, MR-1061-AF, 1999. As of June 16, 2010:
http://www.rand.org/pubs/monograph_reports/MR1061/

Caroe, Olaf, *The Pathans 550 B.C.–A.D. 1957*, London: Macmillan, 1962.

Chivvis, Christopher S., "Recasting NATO's Strategic Concept: Possible Directions for the United States," Santa Monica, Calif.: RAND Corporation, OP-280-AF, 2009. As of June 21, 2010:
http://www.rand.org/pubs/occasional_papers/OP280/

Cohen, Roger, "Over There; Why the Yanks Are Going. Yet Again," *New York Times*, November 26, 1995. As of March 30, 2009:
http://www.nytimes.com/1995/11/26/weekinreview/over-there-why-the-yanks-are-going-yet-again.html

Collins, Joseph J., "Afghanistan: The Path to Victory," *Joint Forces Quarterly*, No. 54, 3rd Qtr. 2009.

Colombani, Jean-Marie, "Nous Sommes Tous Américains [We Are All Americans]," *Le Monde*, September 12, 2001.

Combined Security Transition Command–Afghanistan, "Afghan National Police Fact Sheet," Camp Eggers, Afghanistan: CSTC-A Public Affairs Office, July 14, 2007.

"Communiqué," Afghanistan: The London Conference, January 28, 2010. As of June 18, 2010:
http://afghanistan.hmg.gov.uk/resources/en/pdf/Communique-final

Cordesman, Anthony H., and Jason Lemieux, "IED Metrics for Afghanistan: January 2004–May 2010," Washington, D.C.: CSIS, July 21, 2010. As of November 1, 2010:
http://defensetech.org/wp-content/uploads/2010/07/JIEDDO-Report.pdf

Coughlin, Con, "Has the West Got the Will to Carry on Shedding Blood for the Afghans?" *Daily Telegraph* (London), January 29, 2010.

Crawley, Vince, "NATO's Jones Says Allies Growing More Flexible in Afghanistan," USINFO, Washington, D.C.: U.S. Department of State, November 29, 2006.

de Rose, François, "A Future Perspective for the Alliance," *NATO Review*, Vol. 43, No. 4, July 1995, pp. 9–14. As of June 21, 2010:
http://www.nato.int/docu/review/1995/9504-2.htm

Dempsey, Judy, "NATO Poised to Take Role in Kabul Security," *Financial Times*, November 12, 2002a.

———, "If Bush Does Not Make Clear that NATO Can Be Involved in Critical Issues, the Alliance Will Atrophy," *Financial Times*, November 20, 2002b.

———, "France Bars Moves for Greater Alliance Role," *Financial Times*, February 10, 2003.

———, "New NATO Force to Be Launched in October: Commander Sees the Need for 'A Vehicle for the Transformation of the Military Alliance,'" *Financial Times*, April 25, 2003.

———, "EU and NATO Bound in Perilous Rivalry," *International Herald Tribune*, October 4, 2006.

———, "NATO Chief Urges Overhaul of Afghanistan Effort," *International Herald Tribune*, November 5, 2006.

———, "Germany Assailed for Training Afghan Police Poorly," *New York Times*, November 15, 2006.

———, "Europe Reluctant to Set Up a Security Doctrine," *International Herald Tribune*, May 10, 2008.

———, "German General Criticizes Nation's Efforts in Afghanistan," *Boston Globe*, December 1, 2008.

Dempsey, Judy, and David S. Cloud, "Europeans Balking at New Afghan Role," *New York Times*, September 14, 2005.

DeYoung, Karen, "Chirac Moves to Repair U.S. Ties; Relations Still Strained Despite French Overtures," *Washington Post*, April 16, 2003.

Dobbins, James, "Talking to the Taliban," *New York Times*, May 11, 2010.

Donnelly, Thomas, "Coalition Still Critical as America Escalates Afghan War," *Washington Examiner*, June 16, 2009.

"Dutch Troops End Afghanistan Deployment," BBC News, August 1, 2010. As of August 11, 2010:
http://www.bbc.co.uk/news/world-south-asia-10829837

Entous, Adam, "US Makes Appeal to NATO on Afghan Training," Reuters, February 4, 2010.

Erlanger, Steven, "For NATO, Little Is Sure Now but Growth," *New York Times*, May 19, 2002.

Evans, Michael, "NATO Mission Accused of 'Wavering' Political Will in Afghanistan," *The Times* (London), October 21, 2008.

Fitchett, Joseph, "NATO Agrees to Help New EU Force," *International Herald Tribune*, December 16, 2002.

"The Frustrated West," *Time*, May 19, 1961. As of June 16, 2010:
http://www.time.com/time/magazine/article/0,9171,872391-1,00.html

Gaddis, John Lewis, *Strategies of Containment: A Critical Appraisal of Postwar American National Security*, New York: Oxford University Press, 1982.

Gall, Carlotta, "Doubts About Karzai Growing," *International Herald Tribune*, August 22, 2006.

———, "U.S. Airstrike Did Kill 90 Civilians, UN Finds," *International Herald Tribune*, August 27, 2008.

Gallis, Paul, "NATO in Afghanistan: A Test of the Transatlantic Alliance," Washington, D.C.: Congressional Research Service, October 23, 2007.

Garamone, Jim, "Training Afghan Army Remains Key to Stability," American Forces Press Service, October 10, 2007.

Gates, Robert M., Secretary of Defense, and Chairman of the Joint Chiefs of Staff Adm. Michael Mullen, "Leadership Changes in Afghanistan from the Pentagon," press conference transcript, Washington, D.C.: U.S. Department of Defense, Office of the Assistant Secretary of Defense (Public Affairs), May 11, 2009. As of June 18, 2010:
http://www.defense.gov/transcripts/transcript.aspx?transcriptid=4424

Gearan, Anne, "More U.S. Troops in Afghanistan than Iraq," Associated Press, May 24, 2010. As of August 11, 2010:
http://www.msnbc.msn.com/id/37324981/ns/us_news-life/

Gilmore, Gerry J., "NATO Must Plan for Future Role, Robertson Tells Ministers," American Forces Press Service, September 24, 2002.

Gliemeroth, General Götz, ISAF Commander, "Interview," *NATO Review*, Winter 2003.

Gordon, Michael R., "NATO Chief Says Alliance Needs Role in Afghanistan," *New York Times*, February 21, 2003.

Government of Canada, Independent Panel on Canada's Future Role in Afghanistan, Ontario, Canada, 2008.

Graham, Robert, and Haig Simonian, "Chirac Cautions Washington Against Unilateral Use of Force," *Financial Times*, August 30, 2002.

Halloran, Richard, "Shultz and Weinberger: Disputing Use of Force," *New York Times*, November 30, 1984.

Hammerstein, Konstantin von, "The Germans Have to Learn How to Kill," *Der Spiegel*, November 20, 2006.

Hitchcock, William I., *France Restored: Cold War Diplomacy and the Quest for Leadership in Europe, 1944–1954*, Chapel Hill, N.C.: University of North Carolina Press, 1998.

Hosmer, Stephen T., *The Conflict Over Kosovo: Why Milosevic Decided to Settle When He Did*, Santa Monica, Calif.: RAND Corporation, MR-1351-AF, 2001. As of June 16, 2010:
http://www.rand.org/pubs/monograph_reports/MR1351/

Hurst, Steven R., "War Weariness in the U.S. Clouds Battle Against Taliban," Associated Press, August 21, 2009.

icasualties.org, Operation Enduring Freedom, web page, various dates. As of June 18, 2010:
http://www.icasualties.org/OEF/index.aspx

International Crisis Group, "Afghanistan: The Need for International Resolve," Washington, D.C., Asia Report 145, February 6, 2008.

International Institute for Strategic Studies, *The Military Balance*, Vol. 109, No. 1, February 2009.

———, *The Military Balance*, Vol. 110, No. 1, February 2010.

Jarreau, Patrick, "America Cannot Understand Being Regarded as 'More Dangerous Than Saddam Husayn': National Security Adviser Condoleezza Rice Harks Back to Disagreement Over Iraq," *Le Monde*, June 1, 2003.

Jones, General James L., "NATO's Role in Afghanistan," transcript of presentation to Council on Foreign Relations, October 4, 2006a.

———, "Update on NATO Operations in Afghanistan," Foreign Press Center Roundtable, Washington, D.C., October 24, 2006b.

———, "Remarks to the Atlantic Council on the Future Role of NATO," December 21, 2006c.

Jones, James L., and Harlan Ullman, "What Is at Stake in Afghanistan," *Washington Post*, April 10, 2007.

Jones, Seth G., "The State of the Afghan Insurgency," testimony presented before the Canadian Senate National Security and Defence Committee on December 10, 2007, Santa Monica, Calif.: RAND Corporation, CT-296, 2007. As of June 18, 2010:
http://www.rand.org/pubs/testimonies/CT296/

———, "Getting Back on Track in Afghanistan," testimony presented before the House Foreign Affairs Committee, Subcommittee on the Middle East and South Asia on April 2, 2008, Santa Monica, Calif.: RAND Corporation, CT-301, 2008. As of June 18, 2010:
http://www.rand.org/pubs/testimonies/CT301/

———, *In the Graveyard of Empires: America's War in Afghanistan*, New York: W.W. Norton & Company, 2009.

Jourand, Erwan, "Chirac Backs War on Terrorism 'Without Mercy' at Francophone Summit," Agence France Presse, October 19, 2002.

Kaiser, Robert G., and Keith B. Richburg, "NATO Looking Ahead to a Mission Makeover," *Washington Post*, November 5, 2002.

Katzman, Kenneth, "Afghanistan: Post-War Governance, Security, and U.S. Policy," Washington, D.C.: Congressional Research Service, September 29, 2008.

———, "Afghanistan: Post-Taliban Governance, Security, and U.S. Policy," Washington, D.C.: Congressional Research Service, December 30, 2009.

———, "Afghanistan: Post-Taliban Governance, Security, and U.S. Policy," Washington, D.C.: Congressional Research Service, July 21, 2010. As of August 11, 2010:
http://www.fas.org/sgp/crs/row/RL30588.pdf

———, "Afghanistan: Politics, Elections, and Government Performance," Washington, D.C.: Congressional Research Service, Septembe 14, 2010. As of November 1, 2010:
http://assets.opencrs.com/rpts/RS21922_20100914.pdf

Kessler, Glenn, "Diplomatic Gap Between U.S., Its Allies Widens," *Washington Post*, September 1, 2002.

Kissinger, Henry A., *The Troubled Partnership: A Re-Appraisal of the Atlantic Alliance*, New York: McGraw-Hill, 1965.

Koelbl, Susanne, "NATO Battles Rising Hostility in Afghanistan," *Der Spiegel*, March 13, 2007.

Kozaryn, Linda D., "'Mr. NATO' Explains Enlargement," American Forces Press Service, April 1998.

Lambeth, Benjamin S., "Lessons from the War in Kosovo," *Joint Force Quarterly*, Vol. 30, Spring 2002. As of August 18, 2010:
http://www.dtic.mil/doctrine/jel/jfq_pubs/0530.pdf

Library of Congress, Bill Summary & Status, 100th Congress (1987–1988): H.AMDT.628, 1988. As of June 21, 2010:
http://thomas.loc.gov/cgi-bin/bdquery/z?d100:HZ00628:

Loeb, Vernon, "U.S. Urges NATO to Expand Role in Afghanistan," *Washington Post*, February 21, 2003.

Lubold, Gordon, "In Afghanistan, Time Is Running Out, Pentagon Worries," *Christian Science Monitor*, June 2, 2009.

MacDonald, Alistair, Matthew Rosenberg, and Jay Solomon, "Nations Outline Afghan Security Shift," *Wall Street Journal*, January 29, 2010.

Mather, Ian, "West Outgrows NATO Paper Tiger," *The Scotsman*, November 24, 2002.

McChrystal, General Stanley A., "COMISAF's Initial Assessment," Kabul: Headquarters, International Security Assistance Force, August 30, 2009.

McCreary, John, "NightWatch," AFCEA Intelligence, July 8, 2009. As of June 18, 2010:
http://nightwatch.afcea.org/nightwatch_20090708.htm

Melenic, Marina, "Craddock Warns Alliance Credibility Is on the Line in Afghanistan," *Inside the Army*, May 21, 2007.

Merkel, Angela, "Strengthening NATO's Ability to Act," speech by Chancellor Merkel at the 50th anniversary celebration of the German Atlantic Society in Berlin, Washington, D.C.: German Embassy, October 25, 2006. As of August 5, 2010 (in German):
http://www.deutscheatlantischegesellschaft.de/cms/upload/positionen/atlantischepositionen2.pdf

"Merkel Rules Out German Role in Volatile Southern Afghanistan," Agence France Presse, November 22, 2006.

Miles, Donna, "Afghan Security Forces Training Makes Headway, Despite Trainer Shortfalls," American Forces Press Service, March 28, 2008.

Nardulli, Bruce R., Walter L. Perry, Bruce Pirnie, John Gordon IV, and John G. McGinn, *Disjointed War: Military Operations in Kosovo, 1999*, Santa Monica, Calif.: RAND Corporation, MR-1406-A, 2002. As of June 16, 2010:
http://www.rand.org/pubs/monograph_reports/MR1406/

NATO—*See* North Atlantic Treaty Organization.

NATO Group of Experts, "NATO 2020: Assured Security; Dynamic Engagement," Brussels: NATO Public Diplomacy Division, May 17, 2010. As of August 11, 2010:
http://www.nato.int/strategic-concept/expertsreport.pdf

"NATO States Wrangle Over Troop Commitments," Agence France Presse, February 7, 2008. As of June 18, 2010:
http://afp.google.com/article/ALeqM5i9OAyLgRuRlOy4oRrcTGwBsN87EA

Naumann, Klaus, "Security Without the United States? Europe's Perception of NATO," *Strategic Studies Quarterly*, Fall 2009, pp. 50–64.

Naumann, Klaus, John Shalikashvili, The Lord [Peter Anthony] Inge, Jacques Lanxade, and Henk van den Breemen, *Towards a Grand Strategy for an Uncertain World: Renewing Transatlantic Partnership*, Lunteren, the Netherlands: Noaber Foundation, January 2008.

Nelson, Soraya Sarhaddi, "U.S. Launches Aggressive Training for Afghan Police," *All Things Considered*, National Public Radio, March 17, 2008. As of June 21, 2010:
http://www.npr.org/templates/story/story.php?storyId=88415340.

North Atlantic Council, "Riga Summit Declaration," Riga, Latvia, November 29, 2006. As of June 18, 2010:
http://www.nato.int/docu/pr/2006/p06-150e.htm

———, "Bucharest Summit Declaration," Bucharest, Romania, April 3, 2008. As of June 21, 2010:
http://www.nato.int/docu/pr/2008/p08-049e.html

North Atlantic Treaty Organization, "ISAF Provincial Reconstruction Teams (PRTs)," undated. As of August 18, 2010:
http://www.nato.int/isaf/topics/prt/index.html

———, "NATO to Support ISAF 3," *NATO Update*, November 27, 2002. As of June 16, 2010:
http://www.nato.int/docu/update/2002/11-november/e1127a.htm.

———, "NATO's Partnerships," Riga Summit Guide, press kit, 2006.

———, "Fact Sheet: NATO Support to Afghan National Army (ANA)," November 2007a. As of January 8, 2008:
http://www.nato.int/isaf/topics/factsheets/nato-support-to-ana-factsheet.pdf

———, "NATO in Afghanistan: Reconstruction and Development," June 2007b. As of July 17, 2007:
http://www.nato.int/issues/afghanistan/factsheets/reconst_develop.html

———, "NATO-Russia Compendium of Financial and Economic Data Relating to Defence," press release, December 20, 2007c. As of June 21, 2010:
http://www.nato.int/docu/pr/2007/p07-141.pdf

———, "Contact Countries," *Bucharest Summit Guide*, 2008a. As of June 16, 2010:
http://www.nato.int/docu/comm/2006/0611-riga/media-guide.htm

———, "Fact Sheet: ANA Equipment Support," February 2008b. As of June 21, 2010 [updates to October 2009]:
http://www.nato.int/isaf/topics/factsheets/ana-equipment-support-factsheet.pdf

———, "Progress in Afghanistan: Bucharest Summit," April 2–4, 2008c. As of August 11, 2010:
http://www.nato.int/docu/comm/2008/0804-bucharest/presskit.pdf

———, "NATO Foreign Ministers Reiterate Support for Georgia," *North Atlantic Treaty Organization News*, August 20, 2008d.

———, "Afghanistan Report, 2009," 2009a. As of August 11, 2010:
http://www.isaf.nato.int/pdf/20090331_090331_afghanistan_report_2009.pdf

———, "Financial and Economic Data Relating to NATO Defence," Brussels: NATO Public Diplomacy Division, February 19, 2009b. As of June 21, 2010:
http://www.nato.int/docu/pr/2009/p09-009.pdf

———, "Fact Sheet: NATO Training Mission—Afghanistan (NTM-A)," October 2009c.

———, "Facts & Figures: Afghan National Army," Brussels: NATO Public Diplomacy Division, December 2009d.

———, "International Security Assistance Force and Afghan National Army Strength & Laydown," December 22, 2009e. As of June 21, 2010:
http://www.nato.int/isaf/docu/epub/pdf/placemat.pdf

———, "Backgrounder: NATO Training Mission—Afghanistan (NTM-A)," Brussels: NATO Public Diplomacy Division, April 2010a. As of November 2, 2010:
http://www.isaf.nato.int/images/stories/File/factsheets-april/Apr%202010-NTM-A(2).pdf

———, "Facts & Figures: Afghan National Army," Brussels: NATO Public Diplomacy Division, June 2010b. As of August 11, 2010:
http://www.isaf.nato.int/images/stories/File/factsheets-june/June%202010-Fact%20Sheet%20ANA.pdf

———, "Facts & Figures: Afghan National Police," Brussels: NATO Public Diplomacy Division, June 2010c. As of August 11, 2010:
http://www.isaf.nato.int/images/stories/File/factsheets-june/Juner%202010-Fact%20Sheet%20ANP.pdf

———, "The NATO Response Force: At the Centre of NATO Transformation," web page, updated June 10, 2010d. As of June 16, 2010:
http://www.nato.int/issues/nrf/index.html

———, "International Security Assistance Force (ISAF): Key Facts and Figures," fact sheet with map, July 6, 2010e. As of August 11, 2010:
http://www.isaf.nato.int/images/stories/File/Placemats/100706%20Placemat.pdf

———, "Strategic Concept," web page, last updated July 31, 2010f. As of August 11, 2010:
http://www.nato.int/cps/en/natolive/topics_56626.htm#1

———, "NATO's Role in Afghanistan," August 2010g. As of August 10, 2010:
http://www.nato.int/cps/en/natolive/topics_8189.htm

North Atlantic Treaty Organisation and the Islamic Republic of Afghanistan, "Declaration," NATO Basic Text, September 6, 2006. As of June 21, 2010:
http://www.nato.int/docu/basictxt/b060906e.htm

Obama, Barack, "Address to the Nation on the Way Forward in Afghanistan and Pakistan," Washington, D.C.: The White House, Office of the Press Secretary, December 1, 2009. As of June 16, 2010:
http://www.whitehouse.gov/the-press-office/remarks-president-address-nation-way-forward-afghanistan-and-pakistan

O'Bryant, JoAnne, and Michael Waterhouse, "U.S. Forces in Afghanistan," Washington, D.C.: Congressional Research Service, March 27, 2007. As of June 21, 2010:
http://opencrs.com/document/RS22633/

Ortega, Andrés, and Tomas Valasek, "Debate: Are the Challenges NATO Faces Today as Great as They Were in the Cold War?" *NATO Review*, Winter 2003. As of June 21, 2010:
http://www.nato.int/docu/review/2003/issue4/english/debate.html

Perlez, Jane, "Pakistan Is Said to Pursue Role in U.S.-Afghan Talks," *New York Times*, February 9, 2010.

Pessin, Al, "NATO Commander Says More Troops Needed in Afghanistan," Voice of America, February 10, 2008.

"Putting Things in Order: In a Dangerous and Unstable World, NATO Finds New Purpose," *Ottawa Citizen*, August 12, 2003.

Rasmussen, Anders Fogh, "First NATO Press Conference," transcript, August 3, 2009. As of June 18, 2010:
http://www.nato.int/cps/en/natolive/opinions_56776.htm

————, "A New Momentum for Afghanistan," *Washington Post*, December 4, 2009.

Ravenal, Earl C., "Europe Without America: The Erosion of NATO," *Foreign Affairs*, Vol. 63, No. 5, Summer 1985, pp. 1020–1035.

Richburg, Keith B., "NATO Quietly Slips into Afghan Mission; First Step Beyond Traditional Bounds," *Washington Post*, December 12, 2002.

————, "NATO Blocked On Iraq Decision; France, Germany Lead Opposition to War," *Washington Post*, January 23, 2003.

Ricks, Thomas E., "NATO Allies Trade Barbs Over Iraq; Rumsfeld: Critics Are Undermining Alliance's Strength," *Washington Post*, February 9, 2003.

Riding, Alan, "Threats and Responses: The Europeans; With Iraq Stance, Chirac Strives for Relevance," *New York Times*, February 23, 2003.

Robertson, George, NATO Secretary General, transcript of press conference, Brussels: NATO Headquarters, June 6, 2002. As of June 16, 2010:
http://www.nato.int/docu/speech/2002/s020606f.htm

————, "Opening Statement," Informal Meeting of the North Atlantic Council at the Level of Defence Ministers," Warsaw, Poland, September 21, 2002. As of November 1, 2010:
http://www.nato.int/docu/speech/2002/s020924a.htm

————, "Speech by NATO Secretary General Lord Robertson to the NATO Parliamentary Assembly," NATO Online Library, May 26, 2003. As of June 16, 2010:
http://www.nato.int/docu/speech/2003/s030526a.htm

————, "The Transatlantic Community: Time for Some Lateral Thinking," lecture, Washington, D.C.: Atlantic Council, March 2, 2010. As of June 16, 2010:
http://www.acus.org/event/lord-robertson-transatlantic-leadership

Rondeaux, Candace, "NATO Modifies Airstrike Policy in Afghanistan," *Washington Post*, October 16, 2008.

Rumsfeld, Donald H., "A New Kind of War," *New York Times*, September 27, 2001.

————, "'21st Century Transformation' of U.S. Armed Forces," remarks, National Defense University, Fort McNair, Washington, D.C., January 31, 2002. As of June 21, 2010:
http://www.defense.gov/speeches/speech.aspx?speechid=183

Rumsfeld, Donald H., with Richard B. Myers, "Secretary Rumsfeld Briefs at Foreign Press Center," transcript, January 22, 2003. As of August 11, 2010: http://www.defense.gov/transcripts/transcript.aspx?transcriptid=1330

Scheffer, Jaap de Hoop, "Closing Press Conference," Riga, Latvia, November 29, 2006a. As of June 21, 2010: http://www.nato.int/docu/speech/2006/s061129d.htm

———, "Reflections on the Riga Summit," *NATO Review*, Winter 2006b.

———, "Afghanistan: We Can Do Better," *Washington Post*, January 18, 2009.

Schmitt, Eric, "Afghan Officials Aided Attack on U.S. Soldiers," *New York Times*, November 3, 2008.

———, "U.S. Envoy's Cables Show Worries on Afghan Plans," *New York Times*, January 25, 2010.

Schmitt, Eric, and Christopher Drew, "More Drone Attacks in Pakistan Planned," *New York Times*, April 6, 2009.

Schmitt, Eric, and Thom Shanker, "General Calls for More U.S. Troops to Avoid Afghan Failure," *New York Times*, September 20, 2009.

Sciolino, Elaine, "Trans-Atlantic Disputes Over Iraq Weigh Heavily on Europeans," *New York Times*, April 2, 2003.

Sennott, Charles M., "Nations Mark Sept. 11 with Mixed Feelings: Much Support, But Some Fault US Policy Course," *Boston Globe*, September 12, 2002.

Sheikh, Fawzia, "Craddock: NATO Must Change Unless Members Boost Political Will," *Inside the Pentagon*, June 28, 2007.

———, "DoD Official: Confidence in Afghan Counterdrug Police Will Grow," *Inside the Pentagon*, October 16, 2008.

Shishkin, Philip, "France Wary of Expanding NATO Peacekeeper Role; Involvement in Afghanistan Raises Concerns Over Mission of Alliance," *San Diego Union-Tribune*, February 27, 2003.

Smith, Julianne, and Justin Wiseman, "Riga Summit Delivers Modest Results Despite Tensions Over Afghanistan," *Transatlantic Security Notes and Comment*, Vol. 2, No. 1, January 2007.

"To Paris, U.S. Looks Like a Hyperpower," *International Herald Tribune*, February 5, 1999.

Traynor, Ian, "Russia Accused of Unleashing Cyberwar to Disable Estonia: Parliament, Ministries, Banks, Media Targeted: NATO Experts Sent in to Strengthen Defences," *The Guardian*, May 17, 2007.

———, "Allies' Refusal to Boost Afghanistan Troops a Threat to NATO, Gates Says," *The Guardian*, February 11, 2008.

Trofimov, Yaroslav, "NATO Plans New Top Job in Kabul," *Wall Street Journal*, January 21, 2010.

Tyson, Ann Scott, "Petraeus Mounts Strategy Review," *Washington Post*, October 16, 2008.

United Nations Security Council Resolution 1386, on Afghanistan and the International Security Force, December 20, 2001. As of Jun 16, 2010: http://www.un.org/docs/scres/2001/sc2001.htm

————, Resolution 1510, on the expanding mission of the International Security Force, October 13, 2003. As of June 16, 2010: http://www.un.org/Docs/journal/asp/ws.asp?m=S/RES/1510

————, "The Situation in Afghanistan and Its Implications for International Peace and Security," September 14, 2010. As of November 1, 2010: http://www.un.org/Docs/sc/sgrep10.htm

UNSCR—*See* United Nations Security Council Resolution.

U.S. Department of Defense, "Progress Toward Security and Stability in Afghanistan," Report to Congress, Washington, D.C., June 2009.

U.S. Department of State, Bureau of European and Eurasian Affairs, "NATO: Coalition Contributions to the War on Terrorism," fact sheet, Washington, D.C., October 24, 2002. As of August 11, 2010: http://www.usembassy.it/viewer/article.asp?article=/file2002_10/alia/A2102403.htm

U.S. Government Accountability Office, "Securing, Stabilizing, and Reconstructing Afghanistan: Key Issues for Congressional Oversight," Washington, D.C., May 2007.

"US Still Bitter Over France's Opposition to Iraq War: Bush Aide," Agence France Presse, May 31, 2003.

Vinocur, John, "U.S. Gives Absolution to Its Allies," *New York Times*, June 2, 2009.

Whitlock, Craig, "NATO Hits Snags on Troop Pledges," *Washington Post*, January 27, 2010.

The White House, "Fact Sheet: NATO Summit 2006," Washington, D.C.: Office of the Press Secretary, November 28, 2006. As of June 21, 2010: http://georgewbush-whitehouse.archives.gov/news/releases/2006/11/20061128-11.html

———, "Fact Sheet: 2008 NATO Summit: President Bush Acts to Strengthen and Expand Our NATO Alliance," Washington, D.C.: Office of the Press Secretary, April 2, 2008. As of June 21, 2010:
http://georgewbush-whitehouse.archives.gov/news/releases/2008/04/20080402-1.html

Woodward, Bob, *Plan of Attack*, New York: Simon and Schuster, 2004.

Younossi, Obaid, Peter Dahl Thruelsen, Jonathan Vaccaro, Jerry M. Sollinger, and Brian Grady, *The Long March: Building an Afghan National Army*, Santa Monica, Calif.: RAND Corporation, MG-845-RDCC/OSD, 2009. As of June 18, 2010:
http://www.rand.org/pubs/monographs/MG845/

Zelikow, Philip D., and Condoleezza Rice, *Germany Unified and Europe Transformed: A Study in Statecraft*, Cambridge, Mass.: Harvard University Press, 1997.